HIKING ST. LOUIS

A Guide to 30 Wooded Hiking and
Walking Trails in the St. Louis Area

COVER PHOTO: Cliff Cave Park

i

HIKING ST. LOUIS

**A Guide to 30 Wooded Hiking
and Walking Trails in the St.Louis Area**

© 1998, 2002 by Evie P. Harris

Maps, Photo Credits, Design: Evie P. Harris
Formatting: Joy Paday
Printed by Express Media
Nashville, Tennessee

Published by Evie P. Harris
4717 Crystal Brook Drive
Antioch, TN
37013

ephaut@juno.com

ISBN 0-9665419-0-1

Third Edition
Fourth Printing

This book is dedicated to my daughters Jennifer and Jill
who have always supported my efforts. And to my grandsons
who I hope someday will love the outdoors as much as I do.

AEG-5029

The Spring House - LAUMEIER SCULPTURE PARK

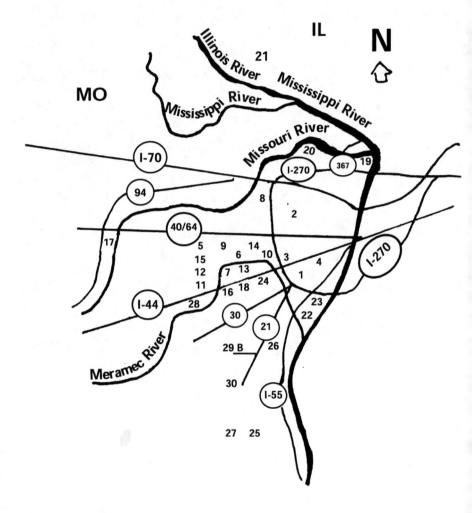

TABLE OF CONTENTS

Page

* Missouri Department of Natural Resources

3

INTRODUCTION

When I originally wrote this book, it was my love for hiking that led me to explore the St. Louis area for wooded trails in the metro area between 4-7 miles. There was no book that combined county, city, state park, natural areas, and conservation areas into one book. Thus, the seeds were planted for the first book. I still feel the trails listed in this book are 30 of the best for the social day-hiker in metro St. Louis.

Some of these parks have upgraded their trails, and others have just made modifications. Still others have recently become official parks with hiking and other amenities. I've updated information as much as possible and added whether pets are allowed or not.

Hiking in the St. Louis area is a unique experience with the many Ozark-like vistas, and four major floodplains. These "wooded jewels" can be a pleasant catharsis in our very busy, troubled world.

State Tree: Flowering Dogwood

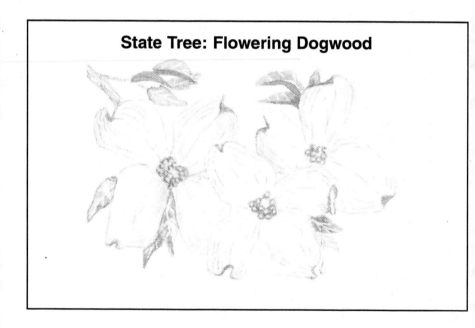

DIRECTIONS ON USING THIS BOOK

For each trail I have included a short description of the main features, as a well as a brief history of the area. I've also given directions to the area, explained how to find the trailhead (the start of the trail) and have also provided a trail map for your convenience. Having hiked several times during the year, I was able to suggest the best season in which to hike. I have also given the following information for each trail:

The telephone number of the agency maintaining the area

Time: Approximate time it takes to hike the trail (round trip) or from point to point, using about 1-2miles per hour, depending on the terrain

Distance: One trail or combined trails in miles

Rating: Easy, Moderate, Difficult-A judgment call based on the steepness of the terrain and length of trail

Disabled-Accessible: Places that offer paved trails and are fairly flat (only noted if accessible)

Restrooms: Where located

Pets: On leash or No Pets

Optimal Season for Hiking: Fall, Winter, Spring, Year Round - Based on vistas, bluff overlooks, plant life, and condition of trails

Disclaimer: The information in this book is subject to change due to development and overuse. I have described the trails as accurately as I could, using maps, park information, a compass, and my watch. These distances are only estimates. Always try to get the latest trail guide and park ranger information before starting your hike.

A lone elk
LONE ELK COUNTY PARK

HIKING HINTS and WHAT TO TAKE WITH YOU
(Some hints I learned from hiking in Colorado)

Socks -   2 pair will prevent blisters
Inside - polypropylene or Capilene to absorb perspiration
Outside - thick, wool and/or other synthetic blend

Shoes -   Good walking shoes for paved trails.
Boots are recommended for better support
on rocky paths and creek beds

Clothing -   Loose and in layers (layers trap air for warmth)
Long pants and/or high socks (tuck your pants in your socks)
Hat recommended to protect you from ticks and sun

Water -   Important year round - helps keep you warm in winter
and cool in summer
Prevents exhaustion and dehydration
In hot weather freeze water bottle and let water
melt while hiking
NEVER DRINK CREEK WATER

Food -   Oranges for potassium, energy, and extra liquid
Any food high in fluid content
Trail mix (the salted kind to prevent dehydration) or any
complex carbs to help keep you warm in winter

Fanny Pack - Recommended instead of a backpack
Cooler and lighter weight
Can easily attach your water bottle to it

Sunscreen - Minimum #15 - Vital on back of neck, face (nose), arms,
legs, and hands

Bug Repellent-<u>Must contain Deet</u> - a necessary ingredient for insect repelling
Use on neck, waist, ankles
Avoid getting off the trail where chiggers are out to get you.

Watch out for poison ivy-"Leaves of three let them be" - both in vines and bushes. A hot soapy shower afterwards should help. Check for ticks at the same time.

THIS BOOK

If you walk often, don't forget to use good stretching exercises.

ACKNOWLEDGMENTS

I am thrilled to write a new and updated version of "Hiking St. Louis." Even though I now live in the Nashville, Tennessee area, I return to St. Louis often to visit my family, and hike as much as possible.

I owe a debt of gratitude to all the rangers and volunteers from Route 66 State Park, Powder Valley Conservation Nature Center, Shaw Nature Reserve, Babler State Park, Ellisville City Park System. Rockwoods Reservation, and St. Louis County Parks Department for their time in helping me with   information.

I owe a special thanks to my daughter, Jennifer who hiked some very difficult trails with me, maneuvering a baby jogger and gerry carrier with 2 small boys.

And, I am indebted to the computer instructors at First Presbyterian Church of Nashville, Tennessee, who offered a weekly computer class and helped me with layout and editing.

And lastly, I want to thank the "Trailblazers" of St. Louis for their ongoing support of my endeavors. After not hiking with them for four years, I just recently ran into them on one of my St. Louis hikes. It was great catching up!

KEY TO MAP SYMBOLS

▲   Trailhead (Start of Trail)

⸴ ⸳ ⸳ ⸳ ⸳   Approximate Trail

♤   Arrow points North

═══   Road

Ρ   Parking

Central-East of I-270
   1. Laumeier Sculpture Park
   2. Malcolm Terrace City Park
   3. Powder Valley Nature Center
   4. Watson Trail City Park

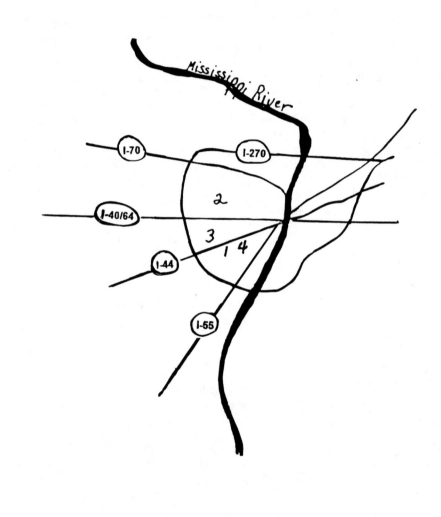

LAUMEIER SCULPTURE PARK
314-821-1209
(Can be combined with Watson Trail Park)

Time: 2-3 hours   **Suggested Seasons:** Year Round
Distance: 3-4 miles   **Restrooms:** Across from museum and in park
Rating: Easy   **Pets:** On leash

Directions: Travel east on I-44 from I-270 south, then east on Watson Road to right on Geyer Road (first stoplight). Continue east and turn left on Rott Road to the second entrance.

In 1986, Laumeier Sculpture Park celebrated its 10th anniversary. Today it has a world-wide reputation for owning the world's foremost program of site sculpture. The original estate was given to the county by Henry and Matilda Laumeier and remained a secluded estate for almost 20 years. The park was enlarged to 96 acres over the years.

Earnest Trova, the world-renowned sculptor, donated 40 large pieces giving birth to the park in 1976, to coincide with the nations Bicentennial. The purpose of the park is to exhibit the broadest representation of late 20th Century sculpture of the highest quality by international standards.

A Blind Maquette Program is in place at the park. Thirteen sculptures have touchable scale models nearby with interpretive information in print and Braille.

Call ahead for museum/gift shop days, hours, and latest exhibits. The sculptures in this park do change periodically. Some are on loan and new ones are added, so there may be some changes from this book.

The trailhead for this walk begins at the southern end of the parking lot down the steps to **(1)Jackie Ferrara's Laumeier Project**, the first piece created for Laumeier. This Mayan pyramid, as some call it, became the driving force for other internationally famous artists. Next, follow the trail to the left, winding around to **(2)Don Graham's Triangular Bridge Over Water**, a unique aluminum, steel, and reflective glass bridge. Pass the **(3)Ursula von Rydingsvard, cedar tubs**. Snow on these tubs create a whimsical scene in the winter. Take the next trail to your left, up and around to the **(4)Mary Miss Pool Complex: Orchard Valley**. This work envelopes a 1920's oversized kidney-shaped pool. and the remains of this 20 acre Hedenkamp estate. Enjoy meandering around the pool and onto the various decks and pavilions.

Return to the main path and veer left to **(5)Beverly Pepper's Cromlech Glen,** a massive earth sculpture which is entered through a narrow gap. You may wish to hike up and view the area from the top. Continuing on, follow the path over the bridge and then left, which will take you to the upland woods. A trail to the left will take you to the lowest part of the park. At the bottom is the **(6)spring house**, formerly used to store food.

(7)David Nash's Charred Wooden Steps Black Through Green will lead you up to the main trail. His philosophy is that decay is park of environmental sculpture itself. Turn left at the top of the hill to get to the open field.

After you pass the **(8)educational shelter**, turn left and pass the **(9)Spirit House.** Keep heading south and you will come to **(10)Meg Webster's Pass a 1-1/2 acre ecological sculpture.**

Begin heading back north in the open field and pick your favorite sculpture. I love the playfulness of **(11)Dennis Oppenheim's Rolling Explosion**, left of the parking lot and the **(12)Vito Acconci's Face of the Earth**, the "happy face" of Laumeier Park, next to the big silver tree. The park's signature piece is **(13)Alexander Lieberman's "The Way"**, which took six years to construct. A large outdoor **(14)stage** used in the '70's and '80's by world renowned conductors is down to your right. Recently it has been used for non-symphony concerts and festivals. Opposite the stage is **(15)William King's Solstice** (which are 5 tall silhouetted figures with arms in different angles).

Across the road to your left is the **(16)"Trova Woods"**. His black poet series is exquisite, especially against a setting of fall colors or stark white snow. However, many of his sculpture pieces are either on loan are or in restoration at this time. **(17)Donald Lipski's Ball? Ball! Wall? Wall!** is a 300 foot long line of 55 marine buoys. And **(18)Jonathan Borofsky's Parts of a Ballerina Clown** is another sculpture over which to muse and chuckle. The musical sculpture in the park is **(19)George Rickey's kinetic Peristyle II?** If you listen closely you can hear the delicate tinkling sound. **(20)Judy Onofrio's I Just Play for Fun** is the arch behind the museum. The origin of the title is in the arch itself.

Have you ever seen a rainbow in a crystal clear blue sky? You can see the rainbow from **(21)Dale Eldred's Sun Field.** Walking from one side to the other you see the colors of the prism, which, in an afternoon can reflect miles away in the sky. Employees of the park turn these solar panels monthly to follow the sun year round.

A children's sculpture garden is in the process of being developed.

Laumeier Sculpture Park is truly one of the great treasures of St. Louis.

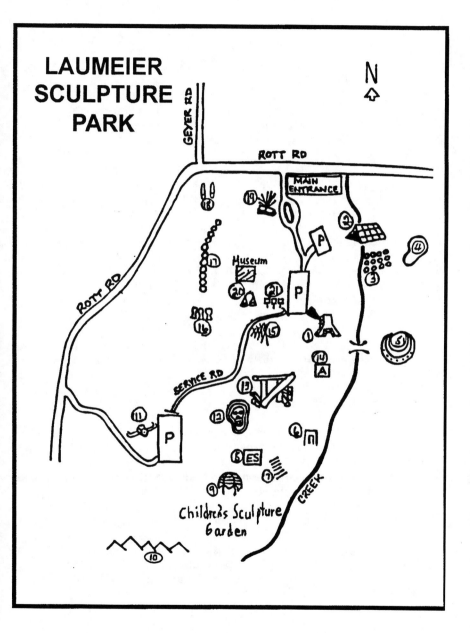

LAUMEIER
SCULPTURE
PARK

GEYER RD

N

ROTT RD

MAIN ENTRANCE

ROTT RD

Museum

P

P

SERVICE RD

P

CREEK

Children's Sculpture
Garden

MALCOLM TERRACE PARK
Creve Coeur City Park
314-432-6000

Time: 1-2 hours
Distance: 3-4 miles
Rating: Easy

Suggested Season: Magnificent in the Spring
No Restrooms
Pets: On Leash

Directions: From I-270 and Ladue Road, turn east on Ladue Road and go 1 mile to Mosley Road. Look for the Creve Coeur broken heart sign, and the name Malcolm Terrace. Turn right on Mosley and go south to St.Paul Street about 1/4 mile. Look for the broken heart sign. Turn right and go to the end of the street, to Malcolm Terrace Park, an urban jewel.

Malcolm Terrace was formerly the site where clay mine workers lived in the 1930's. The city of Creve Coeur began development of the park in the late 1950's. It is known as a passive park, in that it provides only quiet activities. This 60+ acres of looped trails backs up to Westwood Country Club.

The trailhead is at the end of the parking lot. Take the trail around, leave the park and continue over a low-water crossing and up to the next fork. Veer right, red blaze, and hike up a small hill **to meadow #1**. Go straight across the meadow and stay on the main path. In a leaf-off period you'll see the grounds of Westwood Country Club several times. Take the **inner** trail to the left. This will lead you to the **green bench meadow, meadow # 2.**

Continue straight across, and go back into the woods. You will shortly come to **meadow #1** again, from a different angle. Take an immediate sharp right down an old asphalt road. At the bottom of the hill is a large open area. Pass the bridge and bear left at the next fork. Always keep the creek on your left. Go straight across the intersections.

At the fork, go left for an extra adventure. This trail will lead you to the bedrock area of the creek. Carefully walk to the right, in the creek a short way, using the large rocks and gravel to walk on, and pick up the trail on the other side. The trees are now smaller and the trails alternate between grassy and mulched. At the first fork turn left, and continue on the meandering trail.

When you come to the first clearing proceed right on the grassy path. Stay on the main trail and go straight at the next fork. Look for a round storm sewer cover on your right at the fork. At the next fork go left. The trees in this area are much smaller now. This grassy path leads up and around to the right. Cross a culvert and come down to a very large clearing. This is the back of Westwood Country Club.

In returning, cross over the culvert again, but then take an immediate left. At the fork go either way as it is a circle which leads back to the creek trail. Carefully make your way back up the creek and find the original trail again. At the first fork take a left up a small hill. Bear right at the fork taking the long trail. Continue straight downhill to the Townsend Street Bridge.

Notice the oddly-shaped very large sycamore tree in the meadow, an easily identifiable landmark. To return home, turn left and walk halfway up the old asphalt road. Take the first path to the right and continue on the path to the trailhead parking.

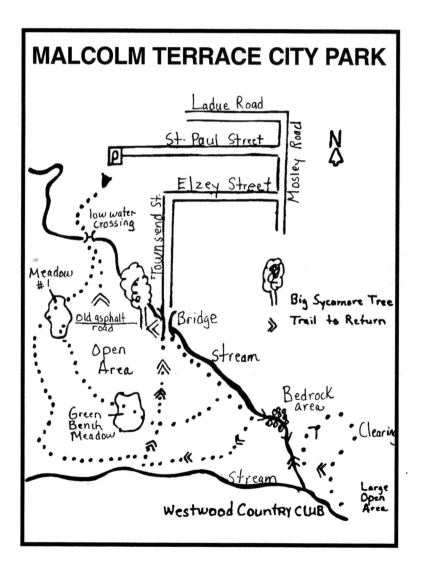

MALCOLM TERRACE CITY PARK

POWDER VALLEY
Missouri Department of Conservation
Nature Center
314-301-1500

Time: 1-2 hours   **Suggested Seasons:** Year Round
Distance: 2-3 miles   **Restrooms:** Nature Center
Rating: Easy-Moderate   **No Pets**
Disabled-Accessible: Tanglevine Trail (1/3 mile)

Directions - Travel south on I-270 to east on I-44, then east on Watson Road. Turn left at the first light, Geyer Road, and turn left on Cragwold, just over the I-44 bridge. Follow Cragwold around to the entrance.

Powder Valley was named for the ammunition stored in this area during World War II. The outstanding Nature Center features many hands-on nature exhibits for children. There is a large wildlife feeding station window, woodland pond which can be viewed from above and below the water level, and many nature activities. The paved trails are shaded and cool.

Tanglevine Trail - 1/3 mile (Disabled-Accessible)
The trailhead for Tanglevine can be found south of the Nature Center by the staging area. This is a lovely easy trail that is open year round.

Broken Ridge Trail - 2/3miles - This trail begins north of the Nature Center in the back of the parking lot. With varied terrain, it is only moderately steep.

Hickory Ridge Trail - formerly known as Trail of Many Creeks - 1 1/2 miles-Begin the longest trail next to the staging area, south of the Nature Center at the long footbridge that crosses the entrance road. This trail is moderately steep, but there is also an optional short loop of 1/2 mile. The trail descends and crosses several seasonal creeks. A savanna has been recently created on this trail.

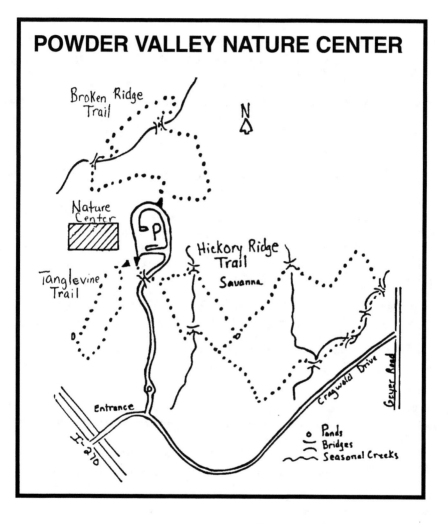

POWDER VALLEY NATURE CENTER

Broken Ridge Trail

N

Nature Center

Tanglevine Trail

Hickory Ridge Trail

Savanna

Entrance

I-270

Cragwold Drive

Geyer Road

o Ponds
Bridges
Seasonal Creeks

WATSON TRAIL PARK
Sunset Hills City Park
314-842-7265
(Can be combined with Laumeier Sculpture Park)

Time: 1+ hours
Distance: 3 miles
Rating: Easy - Moderate

Suggested Seasons: Year Round
Restrooms: Close to Parking Lot
Pets: On leash

Directions: From I-270 south, travel east on Watson Road one mile to Lindbergh Boulevard. Turn right and proceed south another mile. Turn right on West Watson to the park entrance on the left.

Directions from Laumeier Sculpture Park: Turn right on Rott Road immediately leaving the park and go one mile east to Lindbergh Boulevard. Turn right and go south for about one mile to West Watson Road. Turn right and then left into the park.

Watson Trail Park had once been the site of the Rowe family estate. It has all the amenities of a city park, plus a lovely wooded mulched walking trail.

The trailhead is next to the swimming pool and the trail makes a gradual descent into the woods. There are disc golf stands along the trail throughout the park. After crossing a small creek and passing some limestone outcroppings, will be an asphalt road and the lake. At the road make an immediate right to continue on up the steep mulched trail.

When reaching the top of the hill, take the first left down into another wooded area. Loop around to the right and go up the hill again to the main trail. Turn left at the top. Continue until you see an arrow directing you to turn left. Turn there and you will come to an open grassy area. Continue straight across the open area and parking lot of the Sunset Hills Government Center/Police Station.

There is another **trailhead sign** where you enter the park again. This trail will lead you past an old gazebo and other remnants of the estate. Stay on the gazebo side and continue on the trail until you see an old wishing well. At the well, take the small trail to the right, pass the well, and cross the creek over a small cement bridge. Turn left down stone steps cross a foot bridge. After crossing the bridge, turn right and continue up the hill on the mulched trail and into the deep woods.

Stay on the main trail in the woods. Just before the playground turn left and stay in the woods until you come to the asphalt trail. This trail will take you back to the lake. When you reach the lake, turn right to stay on the wooded side. Take the small trail back into the woods right behind the playground. Or, continue on the asphalt trail across the small dam to find the wooded trail on the right for your return to the parking lot.

WATSON TRAIL CITY PARK

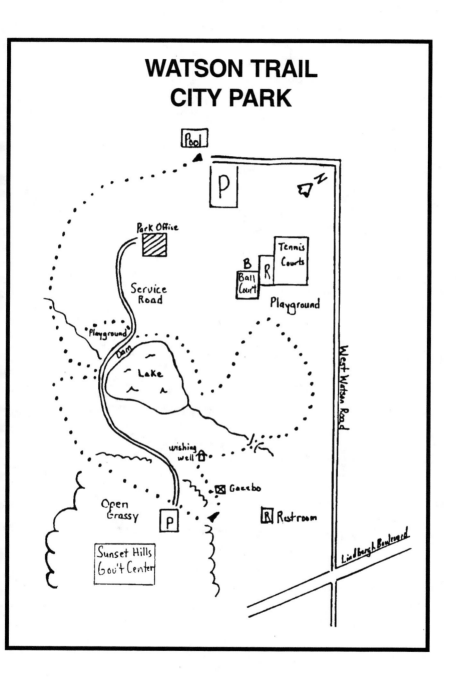

Central - West of I-270

5. Babler State Park
6. Castlewood State Park
7. Chubb Trail
8. Creve Coeur County Park
9. Ellisville Trail System
10. Emmenegger Nature Park
11. Greenrock I
12. Greenrock II
13. Lone Elk County Park
14. Queeny County Park
15. Rockwoods Reservation
16. Route 66 State Park
17. Weldon Spring Conservation Area
18. West Tyson County Park

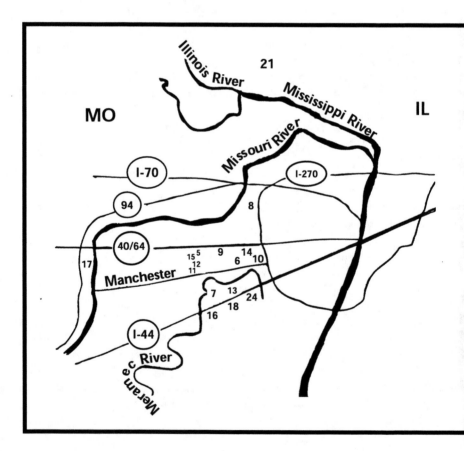

(See page 26)
Dripping Spring - Creve Coeur Park - Winter

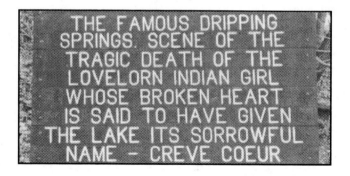

THE FAMOUS DRIPPING
SPRINGS. SCENE OF THE
TRAGIC DEATH OF THE
LOVELORN INDIAN GIRL
WHOSE BROKEN HEART
IS SAID TO HAVE GIVEN
THE LAKE ITS SORROWFUL
NAME - CREVE COEUR

BABLER STATE PARK
636-458-3813

Time: 2-4 hours
Distance: 2-8 miles
Rating: Easy-Moderate

Suggested Seasons: Fall, Spring
Restrooms: Visitor Center and various
shelters and campgrounds
Pets: On leash

Directions: From I-270 south, exit right, (west) on Manchester Road. Travel about 10 miles to Highway 109 and proceed right (north) for 3.5 miles to park on left. Watch for left turn after 1.5 miles. The Visitor Center, about 1 mile from the entrance, will provide current park information.

Babler State Park has an interesting history. In 1930, the two brothers of Edmund Babler gave the state 1,800 acres and over $2 million. This trust was to be used for perpetual upkeep of the park in Edmund's memory. German and Italian prisoners from WWII were also housed here in the many Civilian Conservation Corps structures. Now Babler is a multi-use park with hiking, horseback riding, camping and swimming and an Outdoor Education Center for the Disabled. The open hilly roads make for splendid biking as well.

The Dogwood, Woodbine and Virginia Day Trails are connected trails. A shuttle could be set up at the Nature Parking Lot and Visitor Center for about a 5 mile hike combining the 3 trails, or each loop could be hiked separately.

To get to the Dogwood Trail (2 miles) trailhead, continue on Guy Park Drive from the Visitor Center for 1.5 miles to the Nature Trail parking area. **The Trailhead** is behind the bulletin board. The trail **(signed with green arrows)** will take you down to the beginning of the loop. Proceed left to do the loop in a clock-wise direction. You will cross several horse trails. Continue till you come to a white arrow pointing left. This will direct you to a small cave and spring, one of 6 in the park. You'll pass the Walnut Shelter. Return the same way and continue over the footbridge.

Follow the green arrows at every T junction, eventually merging with the horse trail and passing the Cochran Shelter. The road will get narrower and rockier as it goes downhill. Look for the trail on the right to return to the woods. It will switchback before crossing the resting log and eventually take you back into the deep woods and your return home.

The Woodbine Trail (1 3/4 miles, signed with blue arrows) also begins at the bulletin board and goes right (south). Follow this trail which merges with the paved bike path and passes the Crystal Spring and historic Civilian Conservation Corps comfort station.

After climbing a long hill, leave the bike path and proceed left over a long footbridge. You will then be on a switchback trail leading to the ridgetop first, then looping back down to the Crystal Spring area again. Or, you can connect to the **Virginia Day Trail** at the ridgetop with a connector trail to the right **(signed with white arrows)**, crossing Guy Park Drive.

The Virginia Day Trail (2 miles, signed with red arrows), recently completed, was dedicated to a woman who gave countless hours to Babler State Park. From the connector trail, take the trail to the right, going in a counter-clockwise direction. After crossing the footbridge, take the connector trail to exit at the Visitor Center. The directions for this trail are for 1/2 of the loop.

For the **Hawthorne Trail (1 1/8 miles)** drive about 1 1/2 miles from the Visitor Center on Guy Park Drive and then Wirth Drive to Alta Shelter (highest place in the park) on the right. **The Trailhead for the Hawthorn Trail** (you passed) is across the road and down the hill about 30 feet. A trail spur will lead you to the loop, which you will take in a clockwise direction. This trail has a scenic view in the fall and leaf-off period.

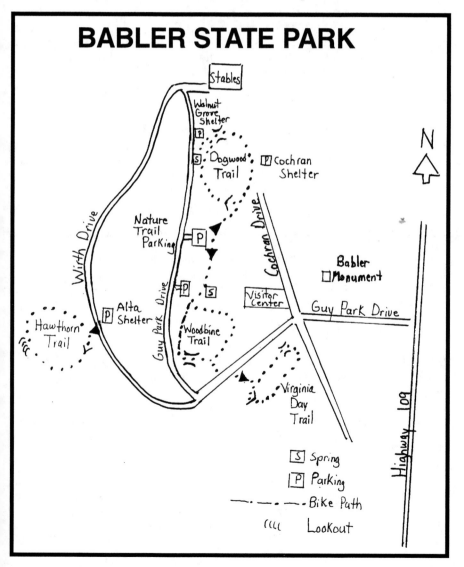

BABLER STATE PARK

Stables

Walnut Grove Shelter

Dogwood Trail

Cochran Shelter

N

Nature Trail Parking

Cochran Drive

Babler Monument

Wirth Drive

Alta Shelter

Guy Park Drive

Visitor Center

Guy Park Drive

Hawthorn Trail

Woodbine Trail

Virginia Day Trail

Highway 109

S Spring

P Parking

— · — · — Bike Path

〈〈〈 Lookout

CASTLEWOOD STATE PARK
Named for the castle-like limestone bluffs
636-227-4433

Time: 2-3 hours   **Suggested Seasons:** Fall, Winter, Spring
Distance: 5+ miles   **Restrooms:** Across from trailhead parking
Rating: Easy-Moderate   **Pets:** On leash

Directions: From I-270 south, go west on Manchester for about 6 miles to New Ballwin Road. Turn left and go south about 3 miles to Kiefer Creek Road. Turn left on Kiefer Creek and go about one mile to the park. The trails for this hike are on the north side only.

Castlewood was a popular beach resort for thousands of people from 1915 to 1950 with weekend clubhouses, saloons and the Lincoln Beach. The beach was on the south side of the Meramec River across from the Lincoln Field. Because many impatient swimmers wouldn't wait for a motor boat to take them across the river, there were many drownings. The river had switched course in 1945 and the entire complex then disbanded. In the winter you can still see some remnants of clubhouses high on the bluff.

In 1979 the state converted it to a beautiful park with 17 miles of hiking and biking trails. It is dissected by the Meramec River. There are breathtaking views of the entire Meramec Valley from the bluff. The low areas of the river trails can be difficult to hike in the summer, because they tend to stay very muddy and the stinging nettle and poison ivy are thick. Mountain biking is very popular on most trails.

Drive past the park office, cross the bridge and go to the **trailhead parking lot** on the right. Begin the **River Scene Trail (2+miles)** at the bulletin board and take it either left or right, the trail to the left being the more scenic. It meanders through a beautiful woods with scattered spring wildflowers until it tops out at the summit. There are benches and bluff overlooks for resting all along the ridgetop. There are more relics of the past on top: clubhouse foundations, fireplaces, and a large water reservoir for public use at the once popular resort. Fork left at the top keeping the river in view.

In making a gradual descent, the **River Scene Trail** connects with a 90-step erosion control boardwalk. When you reach the railroad tracks at the bottom, walk through an underpass and turn right to begin the **Stinging Nettle Trail, (3 mile loop)**. The trail follows alongside the river for about 1 1/2 miles. In late April, Spring Beauty flowers are so thick the ground looks snow-covered. Sweet Williams, bluebells and marsh buttercups are also abundant in this floodplain area in the spring.

After making the turn, the railroad will eventually be on left and the trail will lead back to the river. After the underpass the trail becomes the **River Scene Trail** again. At the open field(Lincoln Field), going to the right will add another 1/4mile loop and eventually come out to the main road. Or, continuing straight 1/8 mile to the main road, and going left under the viaduct will lead back to the trailhead parking.

The **Gropeter Trail** is a 3 mile loop that begins across from the equestrian parking lot and leads into the hills on the north side of Kiefer Creek Road. It has various cutoffs for shorter loops. Check with the park office for more information on the Gropeter Trail.

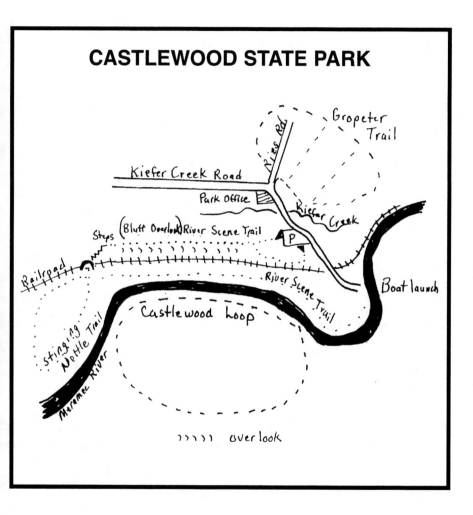

CASTLEWOOD STATE PARK

CHUBB TRAIL
West Tyson County Park
Castlewood State Park
Lone Elk County Park
314-889-2863

Time: 4 hours   **Suggested Seasons**: Fall and Winter
Distance: 7-8 miles   **Restrooms:** West Tyson
Rating: Difficult   **Pets:** On leash
A shuttle required from West Tyson to Lone Elk

Directions: From I-270 travel west on I-44 for about 10 miles to the Lewis Road exit, which becomes the North/ West Outer Road. Turn left for about 50 feet and then right into West Tyson. Continue up the hill to the Chubb Shelter.

The Chubb Trail is a very scenic, hilly and rugged point-to-point hike through three parks. Named for R.Walston Chubb, who formed the Open Space Council in 1965, the Chubb Trail can be hiked from either direction. Directions are given from West Tyson to Lone Elk. The trail is open to hikers, equestrians and mountain bikers, and is marked with yellow arrows at all intersections and at all points of possible confusion.

The Chubb Trailhead is at the Chubb Shelter and begins with a gradual climb up a rocky path. The well-defined trail alternates between switchbacks and rather steep climbs. After about 1+ hours into the hike you will come to a large limestone outcropping. Then the trail comes to a magnificent overlook of the Castlewood Loop and Meramec Valley below.

Follow the trail down and take the path through the valley. When you come to the high water route, you can decide if you want the shorter or longer hike. The low water path will add an extra mile and follows alongside the Meramec River.

At the Castlewood intersection you can make the choice of a longer or shorter hike. Going right and paralleling the railroad tracks will shorten the trail by about one mile. Or walking alongside the Meramec River, the hike will be more scenic and longer. The floodplain flowers are beautiful in the spring and fall. The trail will eventually make a climb out of the river bottom to a wide gravel path which will lead up a hill and back to Lone Elk County Park.

CHUBB TRAIL

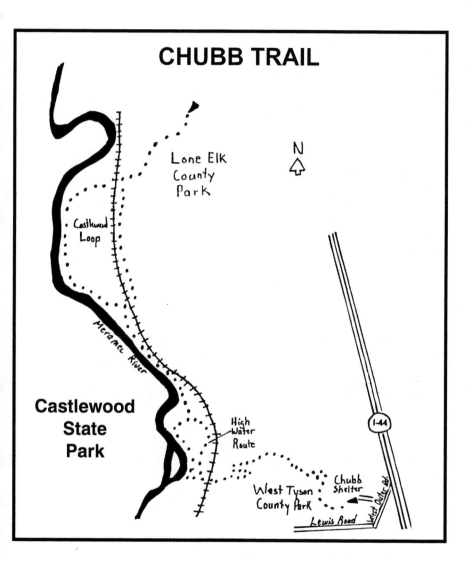

CREVE COEUR PARK
(Broken Heart)
St.Louis County
314-615-7275

Time: 2 hours
Distance: Almost 6 miles round trip
Rating: Easy

Suggested Seasons: Year Round
Restrooms: At first entrance on left
Pets: On leash

Directions: Travel west on Dorsett Road from I-270 for 1.5 miles and turn right on Marine Avenue for the .5 mile descent to the lake. Turn left at the first parking lot, and continue back to the Taco Bell Shelter to begin the walk where you will find the romantic Dripping Spring.

The wide asphalt trail can be used by anything non-motorized and will eventually surround the lake when the Page Avenue extension is complete. The oxbow-shaped lake, a remnant of the Missouri River, is the largest natural lake in the state and has an island in the center. Herons, Egrets, Bald Eagles and other migratory waterfowl can be seen here frequently.

In the late 1800's, for 30 years, Creve Coeur Lake was the home of the St. Louis County Fair for one week before Labor Day. It was also a popular resort with hotels, saloons and even a floating pavilion used for dancing. Light rail service was available here until the 1920's. In 1945 it was dedicated as a county park. Many boating events take place here today, as well as being the home of the St. Louis Rowing Club.

Begin walking on the paved trail next to the lake at the end of the parking lot. From the Taco Bell Shelter to the St. Louis Rowing Club is exactly one mile. Continue across the bridge over Creve Coeur Creek and through a wooded area. After making the bend to the left, parallel the Rock Island Railroad and Creve Coeur Mill Road. When you come to the loop go either way.

The upper park off Dorsett Road contains a baseball field, tennis courts and many picnic areas. The Greensfelder Lookout off Marine Road has restrooms and picnic areas. It overlooks the entire picturesque valley below.

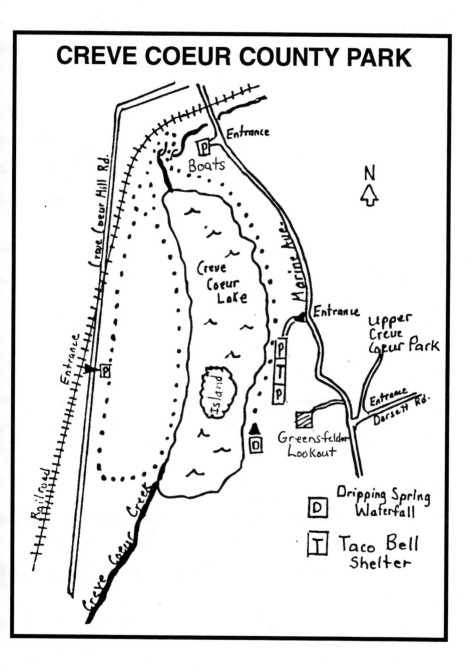

CREVE COEUR COUNTY PARK

Entrance

N

Creve Coeur Hill Rd.

Boats

Creve Coeur Lake

Island

Marine Ave.

Entrance

Upper Creve Coeur Park

Entrance

Entrance
Dorsett Rd.

Greensfelder Lookout

Railroad

Creve Coeur Creek

D Dripping Spring Waterfall

T Taco Bell Shelter

ELLISVILLE CITY PARK SYSTEM
636-227-7508

Distance: 4-7 miles
Time: 2-3 hours
Rating: Easy-Moderate

Suggested Seasons: Year Round
Restrooms: At the swimming
pool in Bluebird Park
Pets: On leash

(A trail system mostly paved, but some parts very steep)

Directions: From I-270 travel west on I-40 for 10 miles to Clarksqn Road. Turn left(south) for about 5 miles to Clayton Road. Park in the Clayton/ Clarkson shopping center to begin the 7 mile walk or optional 3.5 miles. Ellisville I is the hike with the trails on the west side of Clarkson Road. The trails on the east side of Clarkson are in Ellisville II. The **Klamberg Woods** can be added to either. A car shuttle can be set up between the Clayton/ Clarkson Shopping center and **Bluebird Park**.

Since it's opening in 1986, the Ellisville City Park system has been an enormous success. It is a shaded, suburban walk on paved trails through seven small wooded linear parks, each named for a Missouri bird. It also includes **Bluebird Park.** The densely wooded **Roger Klamberg Woods** within **Bluebird Park** is also worth exploring An interpretive brochure obtained from the park office can be used on this 7/10 mile trail which connects to the fitness trail. Additional linear parks have been proposed to be added in the near future.

Begin on Wren Trail behind the Daniel Boone County library branch and continue through several residential areas, enjoying the lovely back yard gardens. Cross Hutchinson Road and stay on Springer Avenue to Clayton Oaks Drive. Turn right at Clayton Oaks and go two blocks to West Field Avenue and turn left. **Quailwoods Trail** is on the left side of the street and follows a creek in a densely wooded area. **Quailwoods** becomes steep at the end and leads out to Virginia Avenue.

Turn left on Virginia to Hutchinson again. Turn right on Hutchinson and then right on Polaris Drive until it dead-ends at **Hummingbird Park**. Take the fork either way. To the right is the longer 1/4 mile steeper trail following the beautiful seasonal creek. The trail to the left is only about 1/8 mile. **Hummingbird Park** exits at Hidden Creek Drive which becomes Froesel Drive. Froesel will lead you across Huchinson again to Weis Avenue, where you turn right. The Ellisville City Hall is at the corner of Weis Avenue and Manchester Road.

Note Barney's B-B-Q across from the city hall, a famous Ellisville landmark. This restaurant, open only on weekends in the summer, has been run by the same family for over thirty years. Eating at picnic tables either inside on a woodchip floor or outside in the fresh air, you will love their smoked-daily meat and family recipe BBQ sauce.

Continuing the walk, cross Manchester and walk south on Pretoria Street to Cathcart Drive. **Whippoorwill Park** begins behind the apartments. Whippoorwill makes a gentle descent. Cross Kiefer Creek Road and enter **Bluebird Park** on the next paved trail.

Continue up the hill to the numbered fitness trail next to the swimming pool. When you get to #3, leave the paved trail and go left down the hill into the woods, passing #4. At #5, cross the paved trail to pick up #6(hard to see behind the trees). Pass #7 and cross the meadow to take the wooden footbridge on the left past #9. Omit #8. Follow the trail up the hill and at #10, leave the woods and make the hefty short climb out to the road. Continue up the road towards the entrance to the **Klamberg Woods**. Or, continuing on the paved path, follow the path between the two baseball fields, on the left, heading north at this point. You'll pass the compost pile and see a green hiker sign. where you'll enter the **Klamberg Trail**.

Enjoy the tranquility of **Klamberg Woods** and take the various trails. An interpretive trail will lead you past an observation lookout where you can enjoy some bird watching. When you're ready to leave, follow the trail to the T junction. Turn right to return to the meadow.

Now, take any path to the right to climb the hill again which leads to the road. At that point, take the paved path between the baseball fields and follow the trail past the compost pile, adjacent to the Carmel Woods Condominiums to enter the **Klamberg Trail**.

This wooded trail leads to Oak Hill Street. Turn right at Oak Hill and pick up the small trail spur on the left which will lead you to Tulip Lane. Take Tulip Lane left to East Meadow Drive. Turn left,(north), and cross Manchester again to Flesher Drive. Take Flesher about .5 mile to the next trail(at the end of Fleisher), **Mockingbird Park (no sign)**. This trail descends gradually and follows a gentle creek. At the valley it becomes **Cardinal Park.** This leads to Marsh Avenue at a footbridge. Cross the footbridge and walk up the hill to Hilltop Drive. Turn right and go to the end of the street to **Woodpecker Park**. Follow it down and exit at Field Avenue. Take Field to the left to complete your walk.

Check with the Visitor Center in Bluebird Park for any updated information.

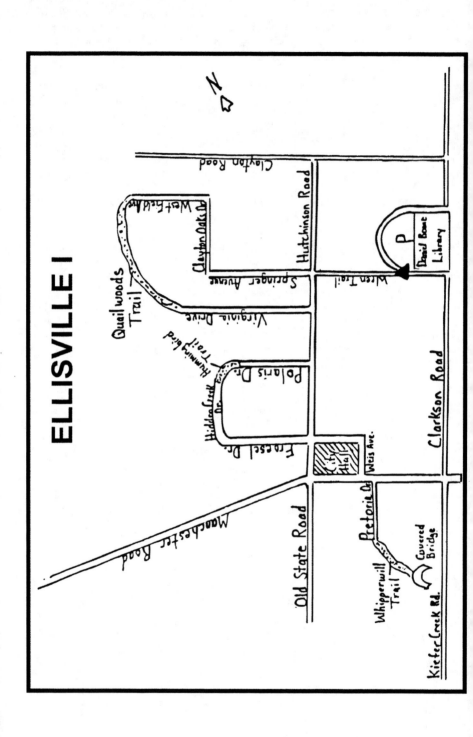

ELLISVILLE I

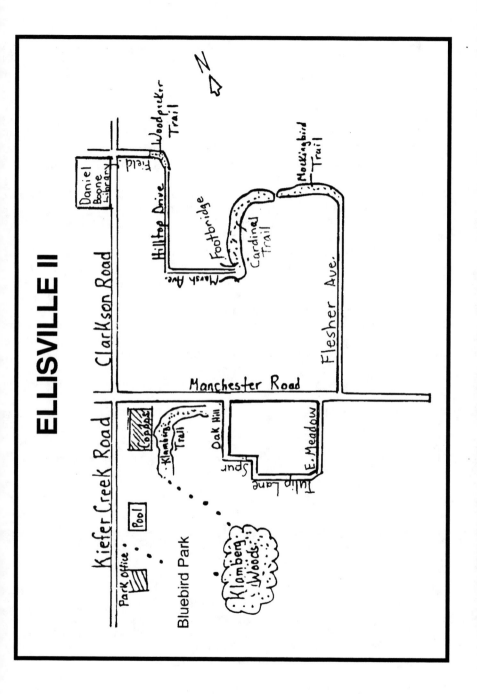

EMMENEGGER NATURE PARK
Missouri Department of Conservation
314-301-1500

Time: 1-2 hours
Distance: 3 miles
Rating: Moderate-Difficult

Suggested Seasons: Spring and Fall
Restrooms: Yes
Pets: On leash

Directions: Go south on I-270 to east on I-44 to east on Watson and left at Geyer Road. Cross over the bridge to Cragwold and turn left. Take Cragwold past Powder Valley (across the I-270 bridge), and turn left. Follow the road to the very end and stay to the right for the back parking lot and trailhead.

Emmenegger is similar to Powder Valley in size, terrain, and plant life but trails are mostly unpaved, rugged and primitive. Emmenegger Nature Park originates from the Lemp family brewery. Their mansion, Cragwold, overlooked the Meramec River and included these 95 acres of craggy, hilly land. In 1971, Russell Emmenegger purchased the area. He gave the land to the city of Kirkwood stipulating that it remains in a natural state and carry his name.

The trailhead begins on a paved path leading to two loops and crossing several bridges, taking you through the lush wooded valley floor. If you want more of an adventure, take the first path up to the right. Slowly make your way to the top, and follow the path to the left, heading north. The trail meanders down and up again and you will cross several wet-weather creeks. Then, you will make your way to the ridgetop again, with the trail getting much steeper as you near the top. If you would like to see the meadow, go straight at the fork which will lead to the summit.

Continue back on the same trail but stay to the right on this outer loop that is now a gentle up and down trail. You are now on the west ridge, going south. You'll pass a series of glades, the first being a butterfly glade. Conditions are just right in this semi-arid glade to attract many butterflies. This scenic bluff area is about 1/2 mile long. To the right is the Meramec River Basin, or as some people call it "Chrysler Valley."

Make your way down several rocky ledges and follow the path to the valley floor and the paved path again for your exit.

An optional path is to begin on the same paved path, but take the second trail up. This path stays close to the valley floor and follows the wet-weather creed, at times. There is lush vegetation here, but the trails are fairly wide and well-maintained. This is an easy trail until you get to the west side. Then, it is a very long and steep climb to the summit where the two trails meet. Go left at the top along the west side and make your way down for the exit.

There are other loops which criss-cross these main trails for even more adventures. Emmenegger is a fun and beautiful place to hike, but be careful of the muddy steep trails in wet weather.

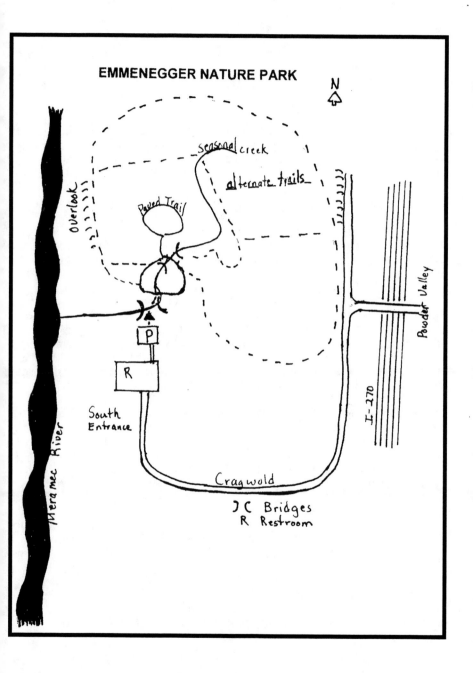

EMMENEGGER NATURE PARK

GREENROCK I
This hike is from Rockwoods Range to
Greensfelder County Park
Missouri Department of Conservation - 636-458-2236
St. Louis County Parks and Recreation - 314-615-7275

Time: 2-3 hours   **Suggested Seasons:** Year Round
Distance: 5 miles a shuttle required   **Restrooms:** (Outhouses) Greensfelder
Rating: Moderate-Difficult   **No Pets**
Topo maps are available at Rockwoods Reservation

Directions: From I-270 south, travel west on I-44 for about 15 miles to the Allenton exit at Six Flags. Stay in the middle lane at the exit. Turn left immediately on Fox Creek Road and continue to drive 1.3 miles to the trailhead on the left.

The entire 10 mile trail runs through Rockwoods Range, Greensfelder County Park and Rockwoods Reservation. Because of it's length and difficulty, directions are given for only the first half, from Rockwoods Range to Greensfelder County Park. **One needs to set up a shuttle from the trailhead on Fox Creek Road and the Greensfelder Experimental Learning Center on Allenton Road, about 4 miles north of the trailhead.**

The Rockwoods Range Tract was formerly a shooting range named for the Rockwoods Military Reservation nearby. In 1943 Albert Greensfelder gave over 1000 acres to the Department of Conservation. In the 1960's the trail was developed by a boy scout troop from Country Day School for a 10 mile merit badge. It is restricted to hiking, horseback riding (separate trails from hiking), and camping. Hunting and mountain biking are not allowed. It has a pristine aura about it which takes one back to the days when St.Louis County was a wilderness.

The Greenrock Trail is blazed from a south/north direction only. It is marked 2 ways: a white blaze on trees and yellow Greenrock Trail signs. Occasionally two trails will be combined, (therefore two colors will be blazed together).

From the Foxcreek Trailhead the trail follows alongside a seasonal creek. It gently proceeds in an uphill northern direction. After about .5mile, the trail makes a long, steep climb. It switchbacks but it is still easy to follow, as it is well defined. After topping out, the trail then follows the contour of the hillside. When the trail comes to a junction, fork right, going east, and then left again. Look for the white blazing on the large trees on the left. Follow the trail around to a widened gravel path and up into Greensfelder Park and the primitive restrooms. Hiking this   distance takes about 1and 1/2 hours.

The Greensfelder Memorial(formerly the Round House) gives some background about the Greensfelder family. The view is spectacular especially in the fall or during a leaf-off period. To return to the trail, look for the white blazing on the trees next to the railroad tie retaining wall.

You will see the yellow Greenrock Trail sign shortly after returning to the trail. Stay on this wide gravel path. (The hiking/equestrian trail going right, down into the woods and to the radio tower, has been omitted in this hike. It doubles back for several miles and is deeply rutted and muddy.)

There is a Greensfelder Memorial sign at the end of the path by Allenton Road. Cross the road to the yellow blaze **Deer Run Trail** and turn <u>left.</u> Allenton Road will be on your left. This will lead you back to the parking lot at the Learning Center on Allenton and Henken Roads.

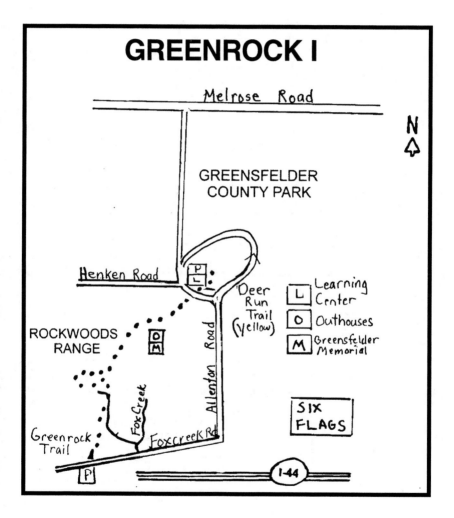

GREENROCK II
This hike continues from Greensfelder County Park to
Rockwoods Reservation
Missouri Department of Conservation - 636-458-2236

Time: 3 hours
Distance: 5-6 miles-a shuttle required
Rating: Moderate-Difficult

Suggested Seasons: Year Round
Restrooms: Greensfelder and
Rockwoods
No Pets

Directions for the shuttle are from Rockwoods Reservation to the Learning Center at Greensfelder County Park: From I-270 south, travel west on Manchester Road for about 12 miles to MO 109. Turn left and go south for about 3 miles to the entrance of Rockwoods Reservation. To get to the Learning Center in Greensfelder Park from Rockwoods, go to the junction of Glencoe Road and Melrose Road (1 mile)from Rockwoods where Glencoe Road becomes Melrose Road. Go to the top of the hill, about 3 miles to Allenton Road. Turn left at Allenton Road and go another 3 miles to the intersection of Allenton and Henken Roads to the Learning Center on the left.

Begin the hike behind the Learning Center on the Deer Run Trail (yellow blaze) **and go left.** You'll also see the white blazing again for the **Greenrock Trail**. At the next junction bear right on **Eagle Valley**(blue blaze),(then blue/white combined). It will lead down to the Carr Creek hollow and a widened cart path(used by equestrians as evidenced by the cross-country fences placed periodically along the path's edge). Cross Carr Creek several times and enter this lovely intimate setting; thick with vegetation, with the creek on your side. Cross the asphalt road and continue to the right, following the (white blazes) in this Carr Creek hollow. The trail narrows, but is still well defined.

The rocky trail then leads up a steep hill where it flattens out and enters **Rockwoods Reservation**. This is a beautiful vista in the fall and winter. The well-marked trail leads gently across Melrose Road and into the **Greenrock Trail**(yellow sign) to continue. There are about 3.5 miles remaining. The trail will then descend down into a hollow again and will cross Hamilton Creek. There are several rises and falls in elevation, and one spectacular vista before making the final descent. The trail crosses Hamilton Creek one more time over a wooden footbridge and exits into a lovely meadow at Rockwoods, just before the Visitor Center.

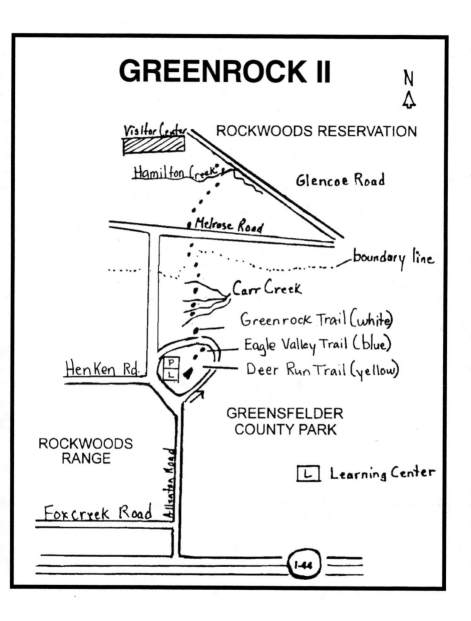

GREENROCK II

N

ROCKWOODS RESERVATION

Visitor Center

Hamilton Creek

Glencoe Road

Melrose Road

boundary line

Carr Creek

Greenrock Trail (white)
Eagle Valley Trail (blue)
Deer Run Trail (yellow)

HenKen Rd.

P
L

GREENSFELDER
COUNTY PARK

ROCKWOODS
RANGE

Allenton Road

L Learning Center

Foxcreek Road

I-44

LONE ELK COUNTY PARK/ CASTLEWOOD LOOP
636-225-4390

Time: 3+ hours   **Suggested Seasons:** Fall and Winter
Distance: 6 miles   **Restrooms:** Visitor Center
Rating: Easy   **No Pets**

Directions: Take I-270 south to I-44 west for 3.5 miles to the 141 exit. Turn right to the north outer road. Follow the Lone Elk signs across 141 and continue west into the park. For the **White Buffalo Trail**, drive left through the gate on Valley Drive and follow it around to the Visitor Center. **For the Castlewood Loop** hike, park on the shoulder of Lone Elk Road just before the entrance.

Lone Elk Park is named for a single bull elk found on the property when it became a park in 1964. In 1966, children from the Rockwoods School District brought additional new elk from Yellowstone National Park. The bison came to the park in 1973 from the St. Louis Zoo. The raptor program moved to a new building near the entrance of the park.

Lone Elk is a unique St. Louis County Park focusing on select native wildlife no longer found in the wild in the state, such as elk and bison. White-tailed deer and Canadian Geese also find the park their home. There are hiking trails, picnic sites, pavilions and an archery range. Hiking is restricted to the elk and deer area only.

The White Buffalo Trail (3miles) trailhead is northeast of the Visitor Center behind the red sign by the road. At present it is a point-to-point trail but eventually will be a 4 mile loop. It is a well-defined, well-marked easy trail with one moderate section near the end by the tower. Walk back on the road, going past the lake. It is quite common to see elk and deer, as the trail takes you where the animals roam freely. Due to controlled burns, the understory is sparse, consisting mainly of delicate bluestem grass, ferns and ground covers.

The Castlewood Loop (3+miles) trailhead begins at the bulletin board on Lone Elk Road. Hike down the wide gravel road taking the Chubb turnoff to the left. Follow this road for about 1 mile. Cross the railroad tracks to the **Castlewood Loop** sign. The trail then becomes a narrower path leading through a prairie to the river. It splits off again to a narrower path leading down into the woods of the river floodplain Looking across the Meramec River you can see the north section of Castlewood State Park. Follow this trail along the river for a 2 mile loop. After a bend in the trail, a small creek will be on the left. Cross the creek at the trail crossing and exit through a tunnel under the railroad tracks. This trail connects to the original wide gravel road. Take it left to go back up the hill and to the point of origin.

LONE ELK COUNTY PARK

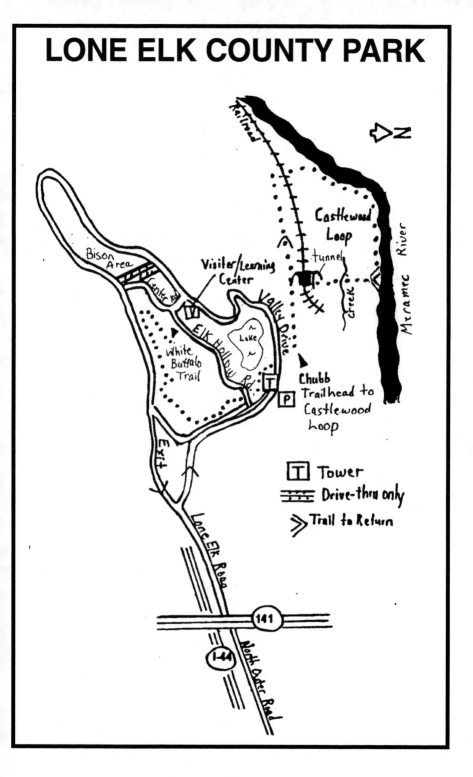

TRAIL NOTES

QUEENY PARK
St. Louis County
314-615-7275 or 363-391-0900

Time: Up to 2 hours
Distance: 5+ miles
Rating: Easy - Moderate

Suggested Seasons: Year Round
Restrooms: Recreation Complex
and portables throughout park
Pets: On leash

Directions: From I-270 travel west on I-40/64 for about 5 miles to Mason Road. Turn left on Mason Road and go south about 2 miles to the Queeny Park entrance/Dog Museum on the right.

Edgar Monsanto Queeny, President and Chairman of Monsanto, Inc. was the last owner of this property. The elegant white estate on the grounds named "Jarville" was his country cottage. Queeny, a horseman and a naturalist sold the home and grounds in 1962, and gave the proceeds to Barnes Hospital. Jarville became a dog museum in 1987.

Queeny Park is now a large multi-use county park. It has 2 ice rinks(indoor and outdoor), tennis courts, swimming pool, state-of-the-art playground, fishing lakes, equestrian trails and biking/hiking trails. The Greensfelder Recreational Complex hosts the summer Pop's concerts for the St.Louis Symphony.

(The directions for this hike are given for steep downhill and moderate uphill terrains.)
Begin the walk on a small footpath connecting the long rows of lilac bushes to the paved trail. Turn right on the paved trail and follow it alongside the split rail fence. This is **Hawk Ridge Trail**. Follow it north, paralleling Mason Road. As the trail changes from paved to unpaved, you will enter an oak-hickory forest. Proceed in this canopy for the next hour, hiking from trail to trail up and down hills. At the first junction, take **White Oak**(lined with white oak and dogwood trees) to the left down a long steep hill. Cross Owl Creek at a low water crossing. Hike up the gradual slope to the next junction, the **Dogwood Trail**. Take this trail to the right, going north again.

The next junction is **Hawk Ridge** again. Take **Hawk Ridge** left and then right, heading to the northern most section of the park. This is a large open field but there are shade trees all along one side of this 1/2 mile trail, including the 200 year old white oak. Pass the equestrian area and continue back in the dense canopy of oaks and dogwoods. At the first fork go left and then right so you will be on **Owl Creek Trail** again. Continue past the park nursery. Cross Fox Run and continue straight on **Owl Creek** for about 1/4 of a mile. This path merges with **Hawk Ridge** in the low area. Pass Jarville Lake and follow the path through the covered bridge. Cross the entrance road and continue north, with Weidman Road now on the left. Follow **Hawk Ridge** north for about 1/2 mile past the tennis courts and Queeny Lake to **Fox Run**. Take **Fox Run** right, going down and then up to exit at **Hawk Ridge** again and your point of origin.

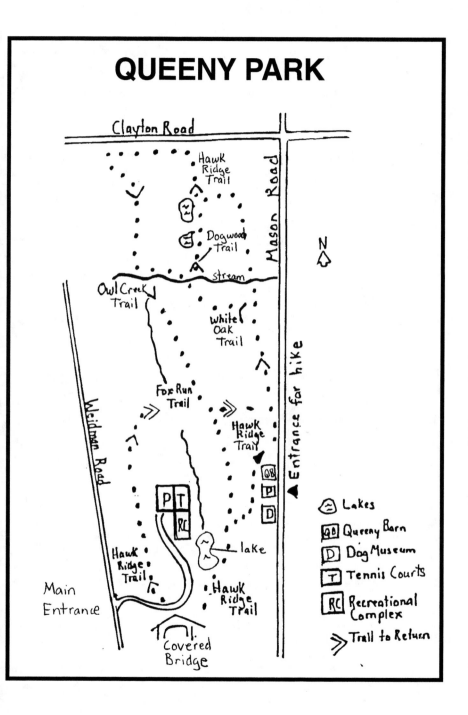

QUEENY PARK

Clayton Road

Hawk Ridge Trail

Mason Road

Dogwood Trail

stream

N

Owl Creek Trail

White Oak Trail

Entrance for hike

Fox Run Trail

Hawk Ridge Trail

Weidman Road

QB

P

D

P T
RC

lake

Hawk Ridge Trail

Main Entrance

Hawk Ridge Trail

Covered Bridge

Lakes

QB Queeny Barn

D Dog Museum

T Tennis Courts

RC Recreational Complex

Trail to Return

ROCKWOODS RESERVATION
Missouri Department of Conservation
636-458-2236

Time: 2-3 hours
Distance: Up to 7 miles
Rating: Easy - Moderate
Disabled-Accessible Trail: Wildlife Habitat (300 yards)

Suggested Seasons: Fall, Winter, Spring
Restrooms: Visitor Center
No Pets

Directions: From I-270 and Manchester go west about 12 miles to MO109. Take 109 left, and proceed south for about 3 miles to the entrance of Rockwoods. Turn right again on Glencoe Road and go about 1 mile to the Visitor Center.

The Department of Conservation bought the old limestone mining settlement "Rockwoods" back in 1938, consisting of a post office, school, boarding-house and tiny houses. There may have been 11 operating kilns in the area, but there are remains of just one today. The establishment of Rockwoods was made possible by A.P. Greensfelder who donated thousands of acres to the state. The Visitor Center is an educational museum with a detailed topographic map of the area and interpretive guides for several trails. Rockwoods has springs, caves, and a huge abandoned quarry, Cobb Cavern, which has recently been closed.

Begin at the **Rock Quarry Trail (2+miles)** on the south side of the Visitor Center. The trail alternates between gradual inclines and level ground. The trail has fewer switchbacks in this area in order to save more plants, therefore the slope is steep at times. Descending the hill, near the end of the trail, is a large ravine for spring-rushing water. After crossing the footbridge turn left. Hike up a steep short embankment and to the entrance to Cobb Cavern. This historic site dates back to the 1800's in the era of limestone mining and is a very photogenic quarry.

The **Trail Among the Trees (1 1/2 miles)** is a beautiful, forested trail with large boulders and caves. **The trailhead** is across from the Visitor Center. It begins in a cool hollow and cuts a path through a rugged area. Not long into the hike are the <u>many steps</u>, and the "bathtub", a small cave on the left. This is a well-defined trail with some hefty uphill climbs in places. This point-to-point trail ends down the road a short way from the trailhead

The **Lime Kiln trailhead** is 1/2 mile southeast of the Visitor Center. It is next to the **Prairie Trail(500 yards)**. Hike the trail in a counter-clockwise direction, starting off to the right of the kiln. Climb about 3/4 of a mile and then level off on the ridge top, for a gorgeous view of the valley. The trail switches back and forth from north to south until it descends into the Hamilton Creek valley. The walk along Hamilton Creek is beautiful with its perpetually-growing watercress.

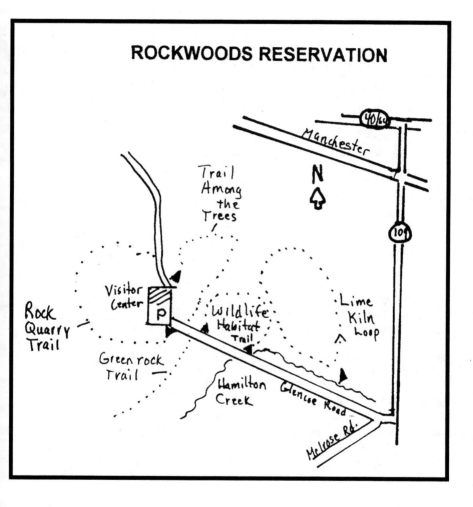

ROCKWOODS RESERVATION

Manchester

40/60

N

Trail Among the Trees

101

Visitor Center

P

Rock Quarry Trail

Wildlife Habitat Trail

Lime Kiln Loop

Green rock Trail

Hamilton Creek

Glencoe Road

Melrose Rd.

ROUTE 66 STATE PARK
1-636-938-7189
1-800-334-6946

Time: 1-2 hours
Distance: 3-5 miles
Rating: Easy (All flat)
Disabled-Accessible

Suggested Seasons: Spring and Fall
Restroom: Visitor Center
Pets: On leash

Directions: South on I-270 to 44 west to Exit 266 at the Meramec River. Stop at the Visitor Center (white 2-story building) and view the memorabilia about the colorful history of the area. The directions for this walk begin at the lower parking lot.

Route 66 State Park opened to the public in 1999, has a colorful history. In the 1920's, route 66, "the Mother Road," was designated as the new federal highway from Chicago to L.A. Roadside businesses were established and the city of Times Beach was founded as a "party place." Then, it grew to a substantial community. Three strikes attributed to its demise: a new interstate bridge was built, the periodic flooding of the Meramec River, and toxic contamination in 1982. After completing toxic cleanup in 1996, the property was turned over to the state. Many of the trees and flowers planted by the residents can still be seen. Many deer, turkeys, and various land and water birds can also be seen.

Begin the walk going east, toward the river, and follow the path left, gong north. You may see eagles in the winter. This "river walk" is approximately 1 mile. You may follow the road all around (four more miles), or return on the same path under the shade of tall oak, hickory, river birch, cottonwood and pine trees. If you take the same road back, go as far as the second last street and turn right. This old road (one of the original roads) will take you under tall trees. This is an excellent place to see many deer. This road brings you out just north of the parking area.

This park is in its initial stages of development. Future plans include a boat launch, pavilion, and a playground. Also, this park will eventually link up with portions of Castlewood State Park in Ballwin.

ROUTE 66 STATE PARK

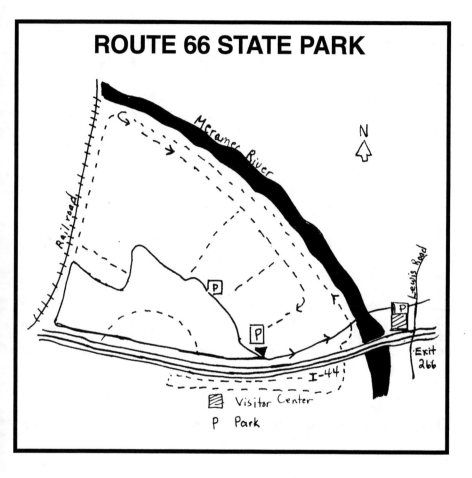

Visitor Center
P Park

WELDON SPRING
CONSERVATION AREA
636-441-4554

Time: 3 hours
Distance - 5+ miles
Rating - Moderate-Difficult

Suggested Seasons: Fall and Winter
Steep trails can be treacherous if muddy
No Restrooms
Pets: On leash

Directions: From I-270 go west on I-64/US40 for 15 miles to Highway 94. Turn left and go south for about 2 miles to the Weldon Spring Conservation Area on the left. There are two trails: the Lewis and the Clark.

In 1796, John Weldon obtained the land and spring through a Spanish Land Grant, for which Weldon Spring was named. During World War II the federal government acquired 17,000 acres in the area for the construction of a munitions plant. Then in 1948, except for the munitions plant, the area was given to the University of Missouri for an agricultural experimental station. The Conservation Department purchased over 7000 acres in 1978 where Weldon Spring is today. The natural area has limestone cliffs that extend one mile along the Missouri River. With its vistas and varied terrain, it is an exciting place to hike.

The Clark Trail is a 5+ loop traversing many hillsides. **The trailhead is at the parking lot**. Begin down a rather wide dirt service road. At the first fork, go right and you will be on a narrower trail. Follow this main trail. Eventually you will come to some limestone outcroppings and an overlook of the Missouri River. At that point you will turn left and begin going down. Continue traversing for about two miles until you come to another beautiful overlook of the Missouri River. Make your way up the rocky path (it is not well marked here) and continue on the path. The trail will eventually lead to the bottom of a canyon and you will be walking in a creek bed. The many hills make it a very challenging hike.

The Lewis Trail - Starts from the Clark Trail in the valley about halfway into the Clark Trail. There is a sign at the junction of the two trails. This extra 3+mile loop follows the Missouri River for quite a way and eventually connects again with the Clark Trail. It is also a very scenic hike.

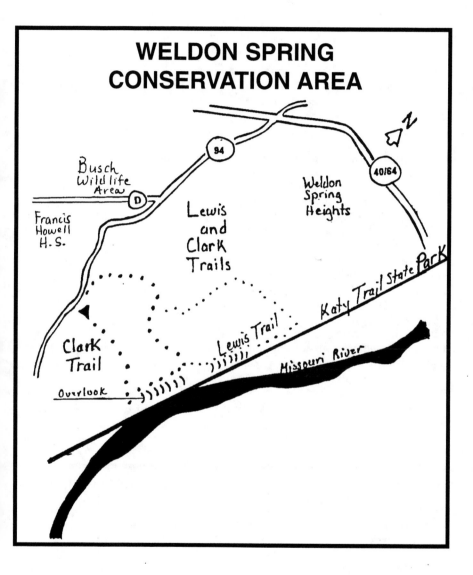

WELDON SPRING CONSERVATION AREA

Busch Wildlife Area

Francis Howell H.S.

D

94

Weldon Spring Heights

40/64

Lewis and Clark Trails

Clark Trail

Overlook

Lewis Trail

Katy Trail State Park

Missouri River

WEST TYSON COUNTY PARK
314-615-7275

Time: 2+ hours
Distance: 3+ miles
Rating: Moderate - Difficult

Suggested Seasons: Fall and Winter
Restrooms: Close to parking lot
Pets: On leash

Directions: From I-270 go west on I-44 for 10 miles to the Lewis Road (Exit 266). Bear right and then left to the North/West Outer Road. Go about 50 feet to the first turnoff to the right into West Tyson. Turn right at the first road, before the Chubb sign, and park at the end of the road in the parking lot.

West Tyson was dedicated as a public park in 1950. The entire trail system is similar to the terrain of the Chubb Trail, densely wooded, hilly and rocky. West Tyson is used mainly by campers, both cabins and tents, mountain bikers (who are riding the Chubb Trail) and hikers.
Colored markers along the trail are not current and so should be not used, and the Flint Quarry Trail is in the process of being re-trailed to complete the 1+ mile loop.

Begin at the Chinkapin, 1 mile trail. You passed the trailhead on your right as you drove into the park. Begin an uphill climb of about 1/8 mile, almost to the ridgetop. The trail levels off and then makes a gradual descent eventually bringing you to a picnic area.

About 20 feet to the right is the Flint Quarry trailhead, a 1 mile loop. There is a short climb to a leveling off and then descends and follows a seasonal creek for a short distance. The trail then makes the very abrupt climb out of the valley and connects with the Chinkapin.

Walk to the right again, up the cabin road next to the Black Oak Lodge for the Ridge Trailhead. This 1/8 mile short, steep trail will connect to the Chubb Trail.

When you reach the **Chubb Trail,** turn left to complete this rocky, hilly 1+ mile great "work-out" trail. Beware of the mountain bikers on the Chubb. Make your way back down the road and around to your car again.

The fifth trail, Buck Run is a short trail spur from the tent camping area to Black Oak Lodge

Although these trails are short you can get a good workout from the steep-up hills.

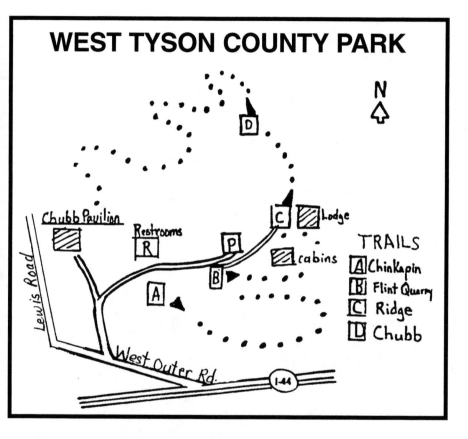

WEST TYSON COUNTY PARK

N

Chubb Pavilion

Restrooms
R

P

B

A

C Lodge

cabins

D

Lewis Road

West Outer Rd.

I-44

TRAILS
A Chinkapin
B Flint Quarry
C Ridge
D Chubb

North of I-270
19. **Coldwater Creek County Park**
    and Fort Belle Fontaine
20. **Little Creek Nature Area**
21. **Pere´ Marquette State Park, IL**

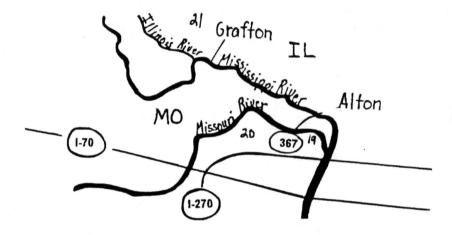

Swinging on a telephone pole at Coldwater Creek

We do not stop playing because we grow old. We grow old because we stop playing!
Anonymous

COLDWATER CREEK COUNTY PARK SITE
314-615-7275
FORT BELLE FONTAINE
(Fort Belle Fontaine Historical Society)
868-0973

Time: 2+ hours   **Suggested Seasons:** Fall, Winter, Early Spring
Distance: 4-5 miles   **Restroom:** Across from Grand Staircase
Rating: Easy-Moderate   **No Pets**

Directions: From I-270 north, travel east about 10 miles to MO367. Turn left (north) about 3 miles and then right on New Jamestown Road. Travel east for about 1.5 miles to Bellefontaine Road. Turn left and go north on Bellefontaine for 1 mile to the entrance of the Missouri Hills campus and K9 Unit. A guard will sign you in at the gate. Drive to the right of the Division of Youth Services and American flag fork to the stone parapet and grand staircase overlooking the Missouri River. Pass the small Fort Belle Fontaine museum on the right, a remnant of the original post.

FORT BELLE FONTAINE is an historical landmark. It was built in 1805 on the low plain near the confluence of the Missouri River and Coldwater Creek. It has an interesting and colorful past as the first U.S. Army Post west of the Mississippi River, an Indian factory, and a campground for Lewis and Clark. Later, it was moved to higher ground because of recurrent flooding. In 1826, the command post was moved to Jefferson Barracks.

Workers in President Franklin D. Roosevelt's Works Progress Administration, in the 1930's, built an enormous, magnificent stairstep complex down the bluff to the Missouri River. You can see what were lily ponds, fountains, and gardens intertwining with the steps. It is in disrepair now but the impressive basic stonework is still there. In addition, there are ruins of bath houses, a fake walled Paris cafe with windows butted up to the hill and huge fireplace dance area.

From the late 1930's to the early 1950's thousands of people flocked to the Missouri River and Coldwater Creek beach via the Bellefontaine light rail. When the Missouri river changed course and modern swimming pools arrived, the beach scene ended. Only the fascinating stonework still exists. From the picnic tables at the top of the hill, you can enjoy a leisurely picnic as you savor the breathtaking view of the Missouri River valley below.

COLDWATER CREEK COUNTY PARK

Begin the walk descending the grand staircase to the unpaved road below and walk left to see the ruins. Take the first path to the right to see the spring which feeds into the Missouri River and gives Belle Fontaine it's name, Beautiful Spring. Back on the main trail, after about 10 minutes of walking, you will see the confluence of Coldwater Creek and the Missouri River. Coldwater Creek will then be about 50 feet to the right of the trail and eventually gets closer.

After passing a swing on the left, made from a telephone pole, and seating up to fifteen adults, the road comes to a shut-ins area in Coldwater Creek. A small ruin bathhouse on the right will direct you down a narrow path on the right into the floodplain area. In the summer there is a dense growth of stinging nettles and tall floodplain grass. Continue on this narrow trail, then climb up the first very steep hill. Just before the second steep hill, take the path to the right. The path leads to a shut-ins, rock out-croppings, gravel bar and canyon area. Eventually you will see the arched bridge used by trains to pass over Coldwater Creek and the guard rail which identifies the end of Highway 67.

Return to the main trail again and take the path up the next steep incline to get deeper into the canyon. This path leads to a very cool, moist, mossy area with large boulders. From the top of the boulders you will see three trails below. The trail to the left will take you back to the main path. Also, take all left and main forks to return to the main gravel road.

Continue on the uphill gravel road leading back to the main grounds. Pass by the St. Louis County Police Dog Kennel, pass "Ozzies", several school buildings and eventually return to the original grand staircase.

A new entrance for Coldwater Creek County Park, north of Coldwater Creek is being planned. At present it is a large compost area.

COLDWATER CREEK COUNTY PARK
FORT BELLE FONTAINE

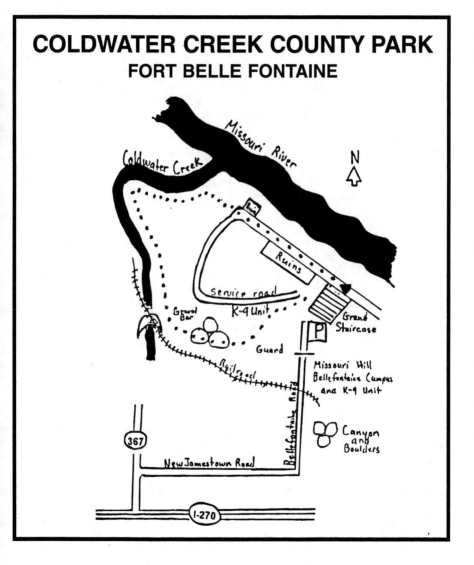

LITTLE CREEK NATURE AREA
Ferguson/ Florissant School District
314-831-7386

Time: 2 hours
Distance: 4 miles
Rating: Easy

Suggested Seasons: Fall, Winter, Spring
Restrooms: At Office
Pets: On leash

Directions: North Entrance (open year round) From I-270 east, exit at Washington/Elizabeth (exit28). Turn left(north) about 3 miles and travel to Derhake Road. Turn right on Derhake and go about 2 miles to Dunegant Park. **Park by the tennis courts and find the trailhead between the large oak trees at the end of the chain-link fence. The trails for this hike originate from the north entrance.**

Directions: South Entrance(open only on weekdays from 9-4 during the school year) From I-270 east, exit at the Washington/Elizabeth (exit28), turn left and go north until just over the I-270 bridge. Turn right on Dunn Road and travel 1 mile to the Little Creek entrance on the left. An official map and additional information about the nature area can be obtained from park office.

Operating since 1972, the Little Creek Nature Area, 98 acres of dense, primitive urban wilderness is one of the largest outdoor classrooms in the country. Five major looped single-file trails and many small trails interconnect to make this a very adventurous hike. Little Creek, a tributary of Coldwater Creek is the main waterway. There are many seasonal creeks requiring six bridges, all named for small animals found in the area.

The ground was once the home of the dentist Clarence Albin who sold it to the Ferguson/Florissant School District. Over the years, the district purchased more land, improved the buildings and developed the trail system. Erosion steps and bridges were built by students of the school district and various boy scout troops. Ethel Nolte, a former science teacher at Little Creek, was one of the spearheads of the program. Now Little Creek contains an office/nature museum, a barn and barnyard, a caretaker's home, and an outdoor building used for science and nature study. There are also an old log cabin and cemetery from the 1800's. Enjoy this "Step Back in Time" as you make your way through "another world".

Enter the woods by the chain-link fence and go left, clockwise, on the Northside Trail. The path is on higher ground, away from the creek in a very dense, low canopy area. The trails are not well marked here, so it is important to disregard any small forks and stay on the main trail. After about a 15 minute walk the trail will lead to **Coyote Bridge** and then **Crow Bridge**. The creek will now be on your left side and the trail will lead to the largest bridge, **Raccoon Bridge.** The trails will be well marked from here on.

Cross **Raccoon Bridge** and bear left on the **Woodland Trail,** passing the lily pond. Now you'll be in an up and down terrain. Stop and enjoy the resting logs at the pond, or continue on the up and down erosion step trail. Cross **Rabbit Bridge** and take the **Nolte Loop Trail** leading to the **Log Cabin Trail.** Bear left and you will come to an old cemetery where six people were buried. The loop makes a bend to the right and crosses the last bridge, **Squirrel Bridge.** The trail becomes wide and mulched, leading past the old A.H.Trampe family log cabin and then exits at the office parking lot.

Walk past the chicken barn to begin the **Woodland Trail** which leads back north again. This trail is partly in a prairie, but then proceeds into a densely wooded area with a large ravine on the left. The trail leads back to **Raccoon Bridge.** Turn left after the bridge to complete the **Northside Trail** loop and exit at the chain link fence.

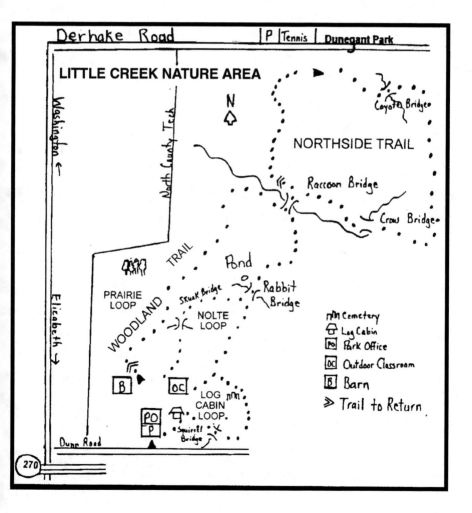

PERE´ MARQUETTE STATE PARK
Illinois State Park
618-786-3323

Time: 2-3+ hours
Distance: 4-7 miles
Rating: Easy-Moderate

Suggested Seasons: Fall, Winter, Spring
Restrooms: Lodge and Visitor Center
Pets: On leash

Directions: From St. Louis take I-270 east about 10 miles to MO 367 north. Drive about 10 miles into Alton, IL. Turn left off the Clark Bridge. Follow IL 100 and the (green)Great River Road and Pere´ Marquette signs for 20 miles. **Enter at the main entrance and then turn left into the first parking lot by the new Visitor Center.**

Peré Marquette State Park, the largest state park in Illinois, has a colorful history, from the early Indians who inhabited the area, to Father Marquette and Joliet who first reached Illinois in 1673. Four miles east of the park, on the Great River Road, a memorial cross marks the spot of their original landing. In the late 1930's, the Civilian Conservation Corps built the lodge and cabins. Inmates from Illinois prisons crafted the large wrought-iron light fixtures and much of the original furniture. The lodge boasts the largest chess set in the world. Hiking, picnicking, camping, and horseback riding are all popular here. Trails are well-marked with color coding blazes on trees.

Goat Cliff Trail-(2miles)The trailhead is at the end of the Visitor's Center parking lot with a faint yellow blaze marking on a tree. The trail parallels highway 100 at first and then begins making a moderate climb. Notice all of the limestone rock outcroppings along the path. The rocks and the boulders become larger and more dramatic as the trail gets higher and steeper. When you reach an opening in the rocks called Fat Man's Misery, it is necessary to climb, around, or over to continue the trail. There is an overlook at the first summit to the left.

Take the next fork to the right on the narrow trail **(hard to see)** and go to the Goat Cliff itself. This is a breathtaking view of Lower Stump Lake and the Illinois River. Continuing on, after you walk through a ravine and reach the next summit, turn right for McAdam's Peak, another spectacular view. The observation platform is a perfect place for eagle watching in the winter months.

Hickory Trail Main-(1mile) **(red)** Go east to the first fork on the right. This trail is very narrow too, and will lead to the **Twin Mounds.** This is a great place for viewing fall colors, and spring flowering trees. Continue on to the main trail and turn left when you reach the junction at the hill with many stone steps. Look to the left for the blaze of **Hickory Trail North.**

Hickory Trail North-(1mile) **(red/white bar)** Walk east on a meandering trail until you reach the junction of **Fern Hollow (orange)** and **Hickory North. Hickory Trail North** to the right is a shortcut back to the lodge. It also leads to the road to begin **Hickory Trail South for about a 30 minute walk back. Hickory Trail South**-(1.5miles) **(white circle in a red square)** There are erosion steps in place for an easy walk back to the lodge.

Fern Hollow Trail-(2.5miles)**(orange)** This trail is a beautiful fern-covered narrow loop through a cool hollow. It is well marked the entire way. The southern side has a vista of a farm field and valley and is very scenic in a leaf-off period. The last .25 mile is a hefty climb until it levels off at the junction with **Hickory South** which leads back to the Visitor Center.

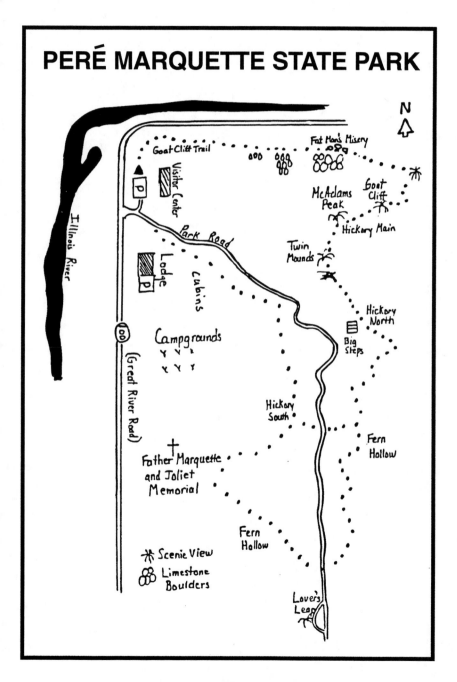

PERÉ MARQUETTE STATE PARK

N

Goat Cliff Trail

Fat Man's Misery

McAdams Peak

Goat Cliff

Hickory Main

Visitor Center

Park Road

Twin Mounds

Illinois River

Lodge

Cabins

Hickory North

Big Steps

Campgrounds

Hickory South

Fern Hollow

(Great River Road)

Father Marquette and Joliet Memorial

Fern Hollow

Scenic View

Limestone Boulders

Lover's Leap

TRAIL NOTES

South of I-44

22. Bee Tree County Park
23. Cliff Cave County Park
24. Forest 44 Conservation Area
25. Hawn State Park
26. Mastodon State Park
27. Pickle Springs Natural Area
28. Shaw Nature Reserve
29. Valley View Glades
30. Washington State Park

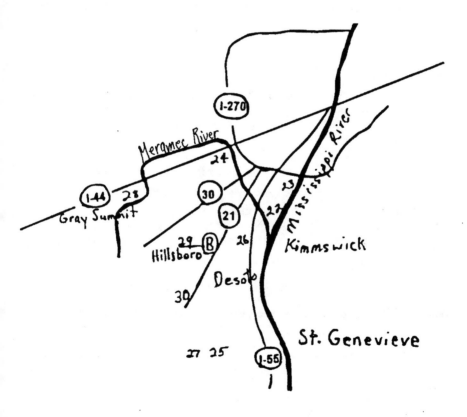

BEE TREE
St. Louis County Park
314-615-7275

Time: 2 hours
Distance: 3-4 miles
Rating: Easy-Moderate

Suggested Seasons: Fall, Early Spring
Restrooms: Across from first parking lot
Pets: On leash

Directions: From I-270/255 south, exit at Telegraph Road. Proceed south for 4.5 miles to Becker Road and turn left. Travel about 1.5 miles to Finestown Avenue and bear left to enter to Bee Tree Park. Use the first parking lot on the right.

In the 1920's, Eugene D. Nims, president of Southwestern Bell and his wife had their Bee Tree summer home built on the Mississippi bluff. Some of the original gardens and buildings are still there today. Now this Tudor mansion is a river museum. One needs to call to check the days and hours the museum is open.

The trailhead for the Mississippi Trail begins at the Lindell Gordon Memorial Garden fountain next to the museum. Walk down the stone steps in the back of the museum, cross the patio and walk down to the eroding grotto to find the connecting path. Follow this narrow trail to the right, with several very steep up and down changes in terrain. This path can be overgrown in the late spring and summer, and possibly difficult to walk at that time. (An alternate trail is the paved service road at the top of the hill, which also parallels the river.)

The trail exits at the Chubb Pavilion, a fantastic lookout over the Mississippi River. Continue on the **Mississippi Trail** again, or walk down the wide gravel road to the **Crows Roost Trail** to the right. **Crows Roost** is about a 15 minute walk.

Continue around the western end of the lake on an undefined path, crossing the spillway and passing the experimental flowering meadow. Cross the chain-link fence footbridge. Once over the bridge take the trail to the left and then circle around to the right to continue to the **Trillium Trail**. **This area can be very wet and overgrown in the spring and summer.** Cross two raised wooden platforms in a cattail/bamboo area. Walk up the erosion steps and bear right to reach the **Trillium Trail**, named for the many trilliums that bloom here in early spring.

Continue to circle the lake until you reach the **Bee Tree/Paw Paw Trails** sign, near the woods. (At this point there are two optional trails). Proceed into the woods but turn left just before the first footbridge to exit on the **Paw Paw Trail** across from the Chubb Shelter, or, continue to the right to experience the entire trail. Return by way of the **Paw Paw Trail** or back-track on the **Crows Roost Trail**.

BEE TREE COUNTY PARK

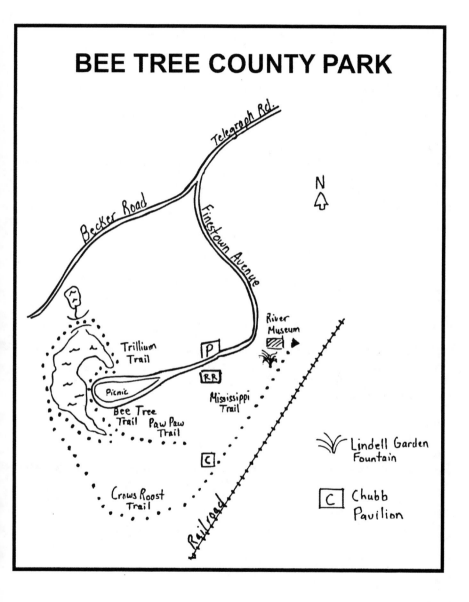

Telegraph Rd.

Becker Road

Finestown Avenue

N

Trillium Trail

River Museum

P

RR

Picnic

Bee Tree Trail

Paw Paw Trail

Mississippi Trail

Lindell Garden Fountain

C

Chubb Pavilion

Crows Roost Trail

Railroad

CLIFF CAVE PARK
St.Louis County Park
314-615-7275

Time: 2-3 hours
Distance: 4-6 miles
Rating: Easy-Moderate

Suggested Seasons: Fall and Winter
No Restrooms
Pets: On leash

Caving requires a county permit

Directions: From I-270/255 south, exit at Telegraph Road. Proceed right (south) about 3 miles to Cliff Cave Road. Turn left on Cliff Cave Road, travel one mile to Cliff Cave Park and stop at the first parking lot.

Cliff Cave Park, consisting of over 200 acres, is the most primitive of all county parks. It consists of a large cave and numerous sinkholes of various sizes. South St. Louis is characterized by a karst topography with no surface runoff. Water seeps through rock and is funneled into a cave system which eventually flows into the Mississippi River. Cliff Cave Park has a magnificent view of the Mississippi River from a bluff overlook on the east side of Cliff Cave Road. The dense oak-maple forest create a thick canopy with colors of brilliant orange and yellow in the fall.

To begin the hike, walk back up Cliff Cave Road and take the trail to the left to the large cave entrance. Years ago this cave was used to store wine, thus the front brickwork. The small cave tunnels can be very dangerous, so take precaution, even with a caving permit.

To hike the trails above the cave, follow the path back towards Cliff Cave Road and hike left up the hill. **Caution: Mountain bikers use many of these trails and may appear very suddenly without a sound. The orange tree markings are for bikers.**

When you reach the top, take the main trail going left. You'll be hiking over the cave when you see boulders below on the left. There are sinkholes everywhere, and occasionally abandoned car parts and entire cars as well. At the first fork, continue straight, and at the 2nd fork turn right, heading west. **At the next 2nd junction turn left, going slightly downhill. Look for an old abandoned car in a sinkhole on the left.** The trail will then bend around to the right. At the bottom of the hill, on the right, is the other entrance to the cave, portal-to-portal. In the afternoon, if the sun hits it right, you can see into the cave. You can also hear the water flowing through.

Proceed up the hill and take the main trail to the left at the top. The main trail then bends to the right at the next fork. Stay on this main trail for about 1/4 mile. It is flat and easy to walk. Pass a large sinkhole lake filled with duckweed. Continue straight at the next junction and pass another smaller duckweed lake on the left.

An important landmark is a large tree split in two, directing you to take the next trail to the left. Note the orange biking arrow on the tree opposite the junction, for bikers only. The narrower trail going left will pass a large double tree and a pecan grove. At the next T junction turn left into a more open area with wild blackberries and wildflowers. Then the trail enters a densely wooded area again with a ravine on the left. Walk down a rather steep hill and cross a slanted limestone shut-in seasonal creek. Cross the creek area and continue on the path leading to Cliff Cave Road.

For a spectacular view of the Mississippi River, walk down the road from where you exited to the 25 mph sign to the **trailhead on the left**. Follow this trail for about 10 minutes to the bluff overlook of the Mississippi River. Return on the same path. A pavilion and picnic area were washed away in the Great Flood of 1993 but will be rebuilt on higher ground in the near future.

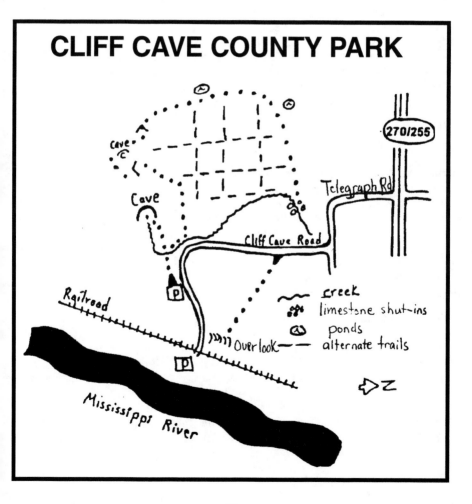

CLIFF CAVE COUNTY PARK

270/255

Telegraph Rd

Cave

Cave

Cliff Cave Road

Railroad

〰 creek
limestone shut-ins
ponds
Overlook—— alternate trails

Mississippi River

FOREST 44 CONSERVATION AREA
Missouri Department of Conservation
636-458-2236

Time: 2-3 hours · **Suggested Seasons:** Spring and Fall
Distance: 4+ miles **Restroom:** At Parking Lot
Rating: Easy-Moderate **Pets:** On leash
Disabled-Accessible: Losing Stream (1/3 mile)
(Check with Missouri Department of Conservation for deer hunting dates in the fall and winter)

Directions: Go west on I-44 from I-270 for about 3 miles and proceed left(south) on Highway 141 to right(west) on Meramec Station Road (first stoplight). Follow Meramec Station Road west to Hillsboro Road (less than a mile). Turn left and then right to the parking area (adjacent to the Kraus horse farm)

This part is outstanding in the Spring, due to the large number of flowering dogwood trees. The fall has spectacular vistas from the horse trails on the north hill. In the late 1980's, this area was about to be developed into custom homesites and commercial buildings. After a four year battle, 300 individuals and 17 organizations persuaded the state to buy and protect it. Now this protected greenspace, also including West Tyson, Lone Elk, Washington University's Tyson Research Center and the boy scout's Beaumont Reservation, is called "the most scenic approach to any major city in the United States."

Begin at the Losing Stream Trailhead for the disabled, at the end of the parking lot and follow the trail around to the first bridge. It leads to a wetland viewing platform. Continue on the **Losing Stream Trail to the right** to access the **Dogwood Ridge Trails, short and long.** These two Dogwood trails are loops and a short spur will connect them to each other at the ridgetop. Take the **Dogwood Trail** to the right, following the stream. The path bends left land enters a large field. It is approximately one mile to the trailhead of the **long Dogwood Ridge Trail.** This wide path is also used by equestrians. After you pass a wildlife viewing platform, pass the short loop trailhead on the left and walk about another 15 minutes to reach the **Long Dogwood Loop.**

Look for a tall stand of pine trees on the left. Cross the footbridge and proceed up the hill. The climb is rather steep for either the long or the short trail. Once you reach the ridge, however, you should feel a cool breeze. This long trail will pass two amphibian ponds that provide habitat for salamanders and frogs. Eventually the **Dogwood Ridge** long loop will connect to the **Dogwood Ridge** short loop. The fork to the right exits back at the creek. The fork to the left exits at the **Dogwood Ridge** trailhead in the equestrian field.

For a longer walk, cross the field heading west, over the creek and up the steep hill to the horse trails. These trails may be very muddy and deeply rutted, but they will provide about 3 more miles of hiking and the vista from the top facing West is spectacular in the fall.

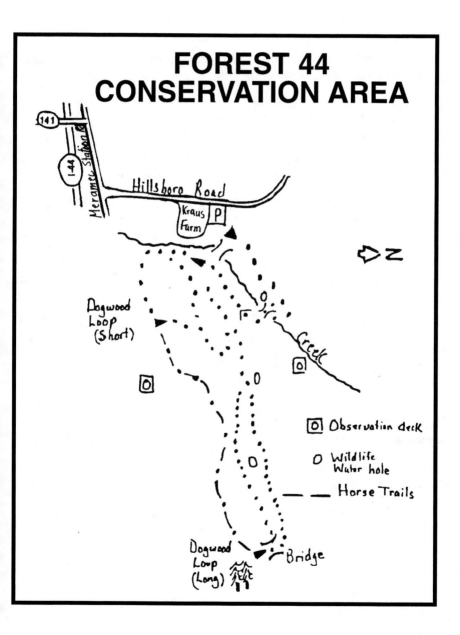

HAWN STATE PARK
Missouri Department of Natural Resources
1-800-334-6946 or 573-883-3603
(Can be combined with Pickle Springs)

Time: 1-2 hours   **Suggested Seasons**: Year Round
Distance: 2 miles   **Restrooms:** At end of parking lot
Rating: Moderate(rocky and steep in places)   **Pets:** On leash

This hike combines one mile of the Pickle Creek Trail with one mile of the Whispering Pines Trail.

Directions: From I-270/255 travel south on I-55 for about 50 miles to Highway 32 (Exit 150). Turn right and go west on Highway 32 about 10 miles to 144, then left 5 miles to the Whispering Pines picnic area. Hawn is about 1 1/2 hours from St. Louis but because of the park's outstanding beauty, it is worth the drive. One does not have to be in great physical condition to hike it, although hiking boots are suggested for the rocky paths.

Named for Helen Hawn, a schoolteacher from St. Genevieve, MO who gave 1500 acres to the state in 1952, Hawn State Park is one of the most beautiful parks in Missouri. The area is characterized by rock formations, sandstone cliffs, canyons, and sandy-bottom shut-in streams. Missouri's only native pine tree grows here, the short-leaf pine. Wild pink azaleas cover the hills in the Spring, as well as flowering dogwood and redbud trees. Many rare plants and ferns are found here. There are 2 crystal clear rock bottom streams: Pickle, and River aux Vases. The forest is predominately pine-oak, but also contains sweet gum, and sassafras. Wild turkeys, white-tailed deer and many smaller animals can also be found. This park has a unique blend of geology and wilderness.

The Pickle Creek trailhead is found at the end of the parking lot·by the restrooms. This wide path follows alongside Pickle Creek displaying the whole shut-ins area. The path becomes narrower and rockier as it slopes up and down. About half-way into the walk there will be a sign that says **"Whispering Pines-10 miles"**. At that point cross Pickle Creek, and continue left with a steep climb, taking you away from the creek. You will now be among the magnificent spring-blooming pink azalea bushes in a less rocky area. Eventually you will approach a knoll and have some beautiful vistas of Pickle Creek that will last for about 1/4 mile. Hike back down and away from Pickle Creek, but at the end of the trail, cross a wooden footbridge over Pickle Creek again for your return to the picnic area.

The entire **Whispering Pines Trail** (north loop-6 mile) and (south loop-4 mile) is worth hiking year round.

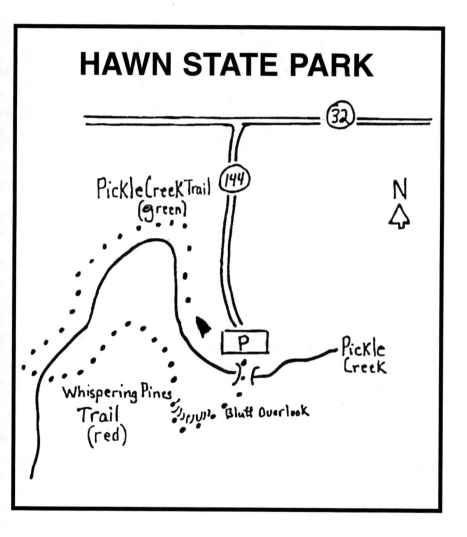

HAWN STATE PARK

32

144

Pickle Creek Trail
(green)

N

P

Pickle
Creek

Whispering Pines
Trail
(red)

Bluff Overlook

MASTODON STATE PARK
314-464-2976

Time: 2-3 hours   **Suggested Seasons:** Fall, Winter, Spring
Distance: 4-5 miles   **Restrooms:** Visitor Center and picnic area
Rating: Easy-Moderate   **Pets:** On leash

Directions: From I-270/255 south, take I-55 south about 30 miles to the Mastodon exit. Follow the signs to the Visitor Center.

Mastodon State Park contains one of the most important archaeological sites in Missouri. Displays in the Visitor Center tell the story of the bone bed through artifacts of bones, teeth and tusks as well as photographs of past excavations. A full size replica of a mastodon skeleton highlights the exhibits. School groups may contact the museum curator for educational information.

The Bone Bed Trail (.5mile) begins at the Visitor Center. It leads to the bone bed, through a wildflower area, across an old quarry, and down a limestone bluff. This short trail is quite steep at the end. Inquire about observing archaeologists at work at the bone bed.

To hike the next trails it is necessary to drive three miles back to the picnic area on Seckman Road. Cross Seckman for the **trailhead to the Limestone Hill Trail (2.25 miles)**. As you begin the loop, take the trail to the right, heading counter-clockwise, as it is less steep. This trail leads along a limestone bluff, past an old quarry, and through a dense deciduous forest.

The Spring Branch Trail (.25 mile) trailhead is found at the parking lot next to the Bollefer Spring. Remains of the Bollefer springhouse are visible along the trail, as well as abundant year-round watercress. This trail is flat and very easy to walk.

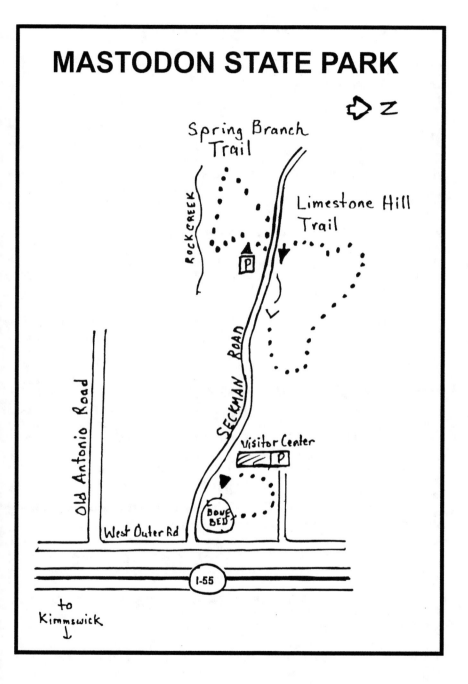

MASTODON STATE PARK

PICKLE SPRINGS NATURAL AREA
Missouri Department of Conservation
314-301-1500
A NATIONAL LANDMARK
(Can be combined with Hawn State Park)

Time: 1+ hours   **Suggested Season:** Spring
Distance: 2 mile looped trail   **No Restrooms**
Rating: Moderate   **No Pets**

Directions: From St. Louis - south on I-55 for about 50 miles to Highway 32. Right on 32 for about 10 miles to left on AA.
Directions: Leaving Hawn - turn left(west) on Highway 32 towards Farmington for about 5 miles to AA. Turn left and drive for 1.7 miles to Dorlac Road and turn left.

Pickle Springs may be called "A Step Back in Time." It is a 2 mile journey past waterfalls, unusual rock formations, a double arch, towering bluffs, and cool canyons. This was the home to mammoths many years ago and you will see why when you enter the cool, wet canyons. Blooming wild azalea shrubs are magnificent around the second week of May.

An interpretive guide is available at the trailhead. The surface of the trail is the same sandy loam as in Hawn State Park and can be slippery in steep areas. From the trailhead proceed in a **clock-wise** direction.

The **Slot** is a series of strange holes and pockets along the sandstone walls. Walls of the **Slot** are continuing to erode from freezing to thawing conditions and the effects of water, air and plants. Walking on, notice the rock pillars called **Hoodoos**. Some are shaped like beehives or giant cauliflower heads. They occur only in this type of rock. Further down the path you will come to the **Double Arch**. It is a special type of buttress holding up a shelf of sandstone which then supports three huge rocks, two of which form another small arch. **The Keyhole** is another type of arch. Can you identify the **Terrapin Rock**?

After crossing Pickle Creek the trail climbs again. The trail then descends and the path leads to the high crossing bridge. Bone Creek supports a lush vegetation of ferns and the northern white violet, an ice age relic. Mossy Falls is a small waterfall in wet weather. This is the halfway point of the trail.

As the ravine narrows, look to the left and you will see horizontal layers of sandstone called cross-bedding. You are entering **Owls Den Bluff** and **Spirit Canyon**. **Spirit Canyon** is a bluff shelter where Indians perhaps camped years ago. The sun never reaches Spirit Canyon, so it remains moist and cool, even on the hottest August days. Scattered along this trail are the small white orchids, rattlesnake plantain and other wildflowers as adder's mouth orchid and partridge berry. Mosses and liverworts also thrive on these shelter walls.

Now the trail climbs to the **Dome Rock Overlook** which sits on the largest hoodoo formation. This is a spectacular vista looking south. The harsh, dry windswept environment support only a few scraggly pine trees which age from before the Civil War.

As you descend from **Dome Rock** listen for Pickle Creek. Pickle Spring is a small spring under the ledge as you face the waterfall. This is a permanent water flow. The spring and creek are named for William Pickles who owned the land in the 1800's. This was the main water source among settlers at that time.

Down the trail from the springs is **Rockpile Canyon**, a group of large boulders that is a result of a collapse in 1959. The crash created a large bluff and a few small arches. Take the short spur to the head of a small box canyon to **Headwall Falls** where you will see more than 20 species of mosses, white violets, ferns, partridge berries and orchids. Toward the ridgetop, enter **Piney Glade**. Because of the poor soil, little can grow here but grasses and lichens. The woodchip trail will return to the trailhead from where you began and experienced the unique " Walk through Time".

Entering "The Slot"
PICKLE SPRINGS

Shut-ins at Hawn State Park

The Keyhole
PICKLE SPRINGS NATURAL AREA

PICKLE SPRINGS
NATURAL AREA

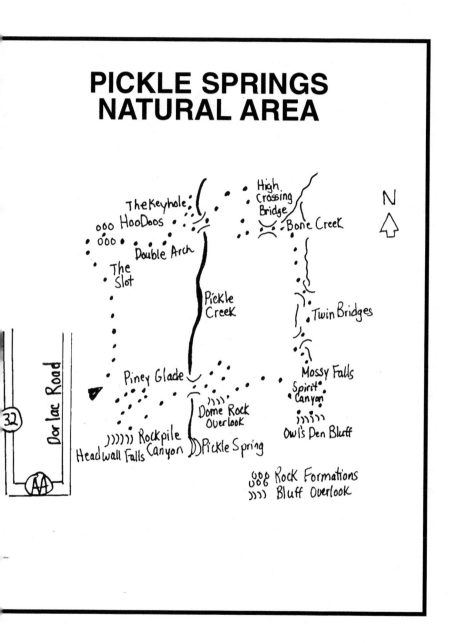

SHAW NATURE RESERVE
636-451-3512

Time - Up to 4 hours   **Suggested Seasons:** Spring and Fall
Distance - Up to 8+ miles   · **Restrooms:** Visitor Center and Trailhouse
Rating - Easy - Difficult   **No Pets**

Directions: From I-270 south, go west on I-44 20 miles to MO 100 at Gray Summit. Turn left and cross the highway bridge. Immediately turn right and then left into the arboretum entrance. Register at the Visitor Center and pay a nominal fee for non-members of the Missouri Botanical Garden. Interpretive brochures and additional maps are available at the Visitor Center where you can also view nature exhibits. Trails are clearly marked throughout the arboretum.

Shaw Nature Reserve, previously Shaw Arboretum, was purchased in 1925 for the purpose of saving the many dying plants from coal pollution in Shaw's Garden in St. Louis. There are approximately 14 miles of trails. Although I have given directions for up to an 8 mile hike, the hike may be shortened in several ways: 1) return to the Trail House and Visitor Center when you see directional signs, or 2) park in various other areas and begin the walk from those points, as at the Wetlands area and Trail House.

Park at the Visitor Center for the trail through the Pinetum forest where the trailhead for this hike begins. Walk down the gravel road that says "ONE WAY DO NOT ENTER" and go to the right on the mowed grassy path (no name) down into the forest. Note the Eastern White Pine sign at the entrance. Follow this path across several wooden foot bridges. Take the second left trail down across the boardwalk and exit at the corktree grove. Cross the long wooden footbridge which will lead to a large meadow. Walk left, continuing south, under the majestic bald Cyprus trees. In the Spring thousands of daffodils cover these hillsides and thousands more are planted each year.

Continue up to the Whitmire Wildflower Garden and gazebo. The newly restored manor house is worth a visit as well. Enjoy the tranquil wildflower garden with it's boardwalk pond and Missouri shade-tolerant flowers. Find the **Brush Creek Trail** down the hill and continue south into the heart of the arboretum. Pass through the deer exclusion gate and cross Brush Creek on stepping stones. Continue through the forest of scrubby oaks and shrubs and take the path that goes to the Trail House.

Once through the cedar woods, the path emerges into a meadow that is being converted into a tallgrass prairie. Continue on this wide path, crossing the service road and passing through a holly canopy to the Trail House where there are restrooms and drinking water. At this point **you are halfway to the river**. The trails from here will take you through an area of ridges and valleys, similar to the Ozarks. **Visitors are required to remain on the trails at all times.**

From the Trail House, continue on the wide path of the combined **Wildflower and River Trails**, marked red and blue. When the trails divide, stay on the **Wildflower Trail and follow** it around. The **#4 marker on the Wildflower Trail** starts the Ledge Trail, per the interpretive guide. The narrow Ledge Trail follows a limestone bluff overlooking what used to be the Meramec River. Many wildflowers grow in this area, due to the constant seepage from above and the rich minerals found here.

Follow this path up to the **Overlook Trail** sign and take it 3/4 mile to the **Overlook**, following the green arrows. Some 650 acres across the river belong to the arboretum as well. Facing the #5 sign, you will notice a small path leading off to the right. Follow this narrow, rocky meandering path down to the **River Trail**. Bluebells, celandine poppies and Miami mist can cover the hillsides here. It is simply breathtaking in the spring.

At the bottom of the hill, in the floodplain forest, go right to get to the gravel bar and then left, passing **"Goliath"** (as I call it) the largest tree in the park which could be 250 years old. Continue toward the river but then take a path left to get to the gravel bar itself. Carefully make your way across the many uprooted trees destroyed by the 1993 flood and continue out to the Meramec River gravel bar.

To return, pass **"Goliath"** again, following the blue blazing on the trees. At the **River Trail** turn right on a wide path for about 1/4 mile to a field and then turn left, heading uphill to the **Spring Trail**. A resting bench is available at the end of a trail spur on the left. Continue on **Spring Trail** up the hill and cross the spring and rocky area. Make the hefty climb back up out of the river bottom area and go right at the top to take the **Prairie Trail** through the cedar woods which leads to the observation deck in the prairie. From the deck you will see a panoramic view of the arboretum.

Take the trail to the right behind the observation deck and hike north through the prairie and over to the **Wetlands** for about 3 more miles. The Missouri Black-Eyed Susan and Indian paintbrush dominate the scene in summer and these prairie grasses grow to be at least 12 feet tall. At the #10 marker in the prairie at the large Hackberry tree, turn left and then right to the trailhead of the **Wetlands**, the newest addition to the arboretum. A side trip leads to another observation deck. Pink and white water lilies and yellow water Primrose are spectacular in these lakes in June. The last lake has a boardwalk with a bench for quiet observation. Notice the beaver island and many beaver trails as you walk around the lake.

After leaving the **Wetlands**, turn right, cross the service road bridge. Instead of turning at the Visitor Center sign, for an extra mile, take the dirt path up to the serpentine wall, where a formal boxwood garden once existed. Walk through the "garden of the past" (follow the mowed path) up to the dam of Wolf Run Lake to find the **Wolf Run Trail**. The trailhead is well marked. This trail will take you directly back through another deer exclusion gate and back to the Visitor Center.

I'm sure you'll agree Shaw Nature Reserve is one of the truly great jewels in the St. Louis area which you would want to visit in different seasons.

It is also a fantastic place to cross-country ski in snowy conditions.

SHAW NATURE RESERVE

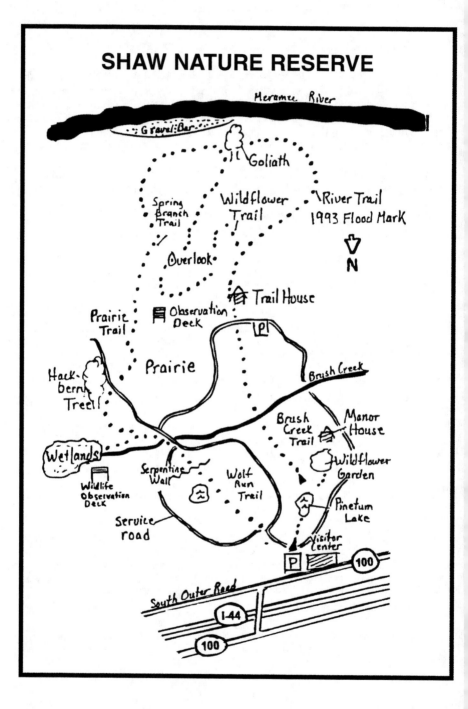

Meramec River

Gravel Bar

Goliath

Spring Branch Trail

Wildflower Trail

River Trail
1993 Flood Mark

N

Overlook

Trail House

Prairie Trail

Observation Deck

Prairie

Brush Creek

Hack-berry Tree

Manor House

Brush Creek Trail

Wetlands

Serpentine Wall

Wolf Run Trail

Wildflower Garden

Wildlife Observation Deck

Pinetum Lake

Service road

Visitor Center

P

100

South Outer Road

I-44

100

TRAIL NOTES

VALLEY VIEW GLADES
Missouri Department of Conservation
314-301-1500
(Can be combined with Washington State Park)

Time: 1-2 hours   **Suggested Seasons**: Spring and Fall
Distance: 3 miles   **No Restrooms**
Rating: Moderate   **Pets**: On leash
(Check dates for deer season if hiking in the fall or winter)

Directions from St. Louis: From I-270 travel south on Highway 21 for about 30 miles to Highway B at Hillsboro Road. Turn right and go west for about 5 miles to Valley View Glades on the right.

Directions from Washington State Park: Proceed left(north) on Highway 21 about 14 miles to Highway B. Turn left and go about 5 miles to Valley View Glades on the right.

The trailhead is to the left of the Valley View Glade sign. The trail is a large clockwise loop zig-zagging in and out of the forest and 200 acre glade area. This glade is magnificent in the late spring with hillsides covered with colors of purple and yellow from the thousands of wildflowers which grow here. Missouri Primrose and Fremonts leather are the most prominent flowers. **In the glade area follow the trail signs closely, as the trail is not well-defined.** You will also cross several intermittent streams as you make your way through the forested portion. This area has much variety of topography and terrain. In returning home, turn right on Highway B to get to Highway 30.

VALLEY VIEW GLADES NATURAL AREA

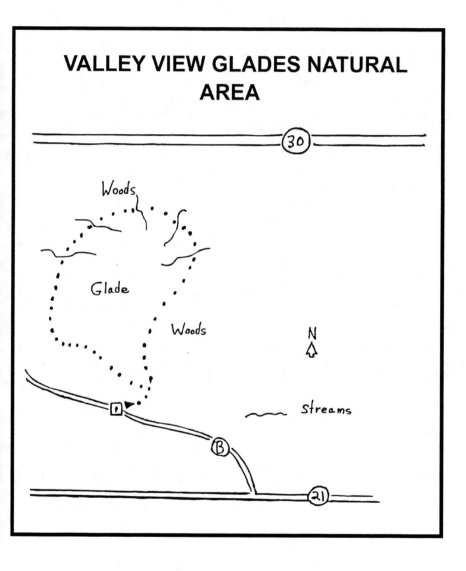

Woods

Glade

Woods

30

N

Streams

WASHINGTON STATE PARK
1-636-586-2995
1-800-334-6946
(Can be combined with Valley View Glades)

Time: 2+ hours
Distance: 4+ miles
Rating: Moderate

Suggested Seasons: Fall, Winter, Spring
Restrooms: Store Lodge
Pets: On leash

Directions: From I-270 go south on Highway 21 for about 45 miles, 9 miles south of Desoto to Washington State Park.

Washington State Park, primarily known for it's three sites of petroglyphs, has three hiking trails and beautiful vistas of the Big River valley. The **1000-Step Trail** built by the Civilian Conservation Corps in the 1930's is worth the effort to hike with it's scenic climb to the top and the view from the Overlook Pavilion. The trails are well marked.

The trailhead for the Thousand Step Trail (1.5 miles) is directly opposite the store lodge. The narrow path leads along the base of a large hill, with limestone outcroppings, waterfalls and dense growth of ferns. **The 1000 Step Trail** begins after about 1/8 mile and proceeds from very steep to switchbacks. About two-thirds of the way is a trail spur on the left leading to the Overlook. Returning to the main trail, and just before the railroad tie steps, you will see a yellow directional arrow on the left. The trail to the summit leads to a picnic pavilion which can also be reached by road. The 1000 Step Trail continues to make the counter-clockwise loop around and then down to the point of origin.

The Opossum Track Trail (3 miles) trailhead is just southwest of the store lodge parking lot across the road at the edge of the woods. It is marked with blue arrows for a clockwise loop. Beginning in a hollow, it crosses a creek several times before making a climb out of the valley. After reaching higher ground the trail passes by the swimming pool and then parallels the road. After crossing the road by the campground area, it heads back downhill into the forest. Parts of the trail overlook the Big River.

The **Rockywood (10 miles) Trail** begins on the northwest side of the dining lodge parking lot. It is signed with orange arrows in a counter-clockwise direction.

WASHINGTON STATE PARK

N

Big River

1000 Step Trail

Overlook

Store Lodge

Bridge

Shelter

Park Office

104

21

Opossum Track Trail

Petroglyph Area

104

To Potosi

TRAIL NOTES

Happy Hiking!

Help keep Missouri's (and all) trails clean.
Leave only your footprints.